MW00335415

"I love love love the book. It's like having a seasoned tutor explaining, well, tricks! I'm learning Python on the job and I'm coming from Powershell, which I learned on the job—so lots of new, great stuff. Whenever I get stuck in Python (usually with Flask blueprints or I feel like my code could be more Pythonic) I post questions in our internal Python chat room.

I'm often amazed at some of the answers co-workers give me. Dict comprehensions, lambdas, and generators often pepper their feedback. I am always impressed and yet flabbergasted at how powerful Python is when you know these tricks and can implement them correctly.

Your book was exactly what I wanted to help get me from a bewildered Powershell scripter to someone who knows how and when to use these Pythonic 'tricks' everyone has been talking about.

As someone who doesn't have my degree in CS it's nice to have the text to explain things that others might have learned when they were classically educated. I am really enjoying the book and am subscribed to the emails as well, which is how I found out about the book."

— **Daniel Meyer**, Sr. Desktop Administrator at Tesla Inc.

"I first heard about your book from a co-worker who wanted to trick me with your example of how dictionaries are built. I was almost 100% sure about the reason why the end product was a much smaller/simpler dictionary but I must confess that I did not expect the outcome :)

He showed me the book via video conferencing and I sort of skimmed through it as he flipped the pages for me, and I was immediately curious to read more.

That same afternoon I purchased my own copy and proceeded to read your explanation for the way dictionaries are created in Python and later that day, as I met a different co-worker for coffee, I used the same trick on him :)

He then sprung a different question on the same principle, and because of the way you explained things in your book, I was able to not simply guess the result but to correctly answer what the outcome would be. That means that you did a great job at explaining things :)

I am not new in Python and some of the concepts in some of the chapters are not new to me, but I must say that I do get something out of every chapter so far, so kudos for writing a very nice book and for doing a fantastic job at explaining concepts behind the tricks! I'm very much looking forward to the updates and I will certainly let my friends and co-workers know about your book."

— **Og Maciel**, Python Developer at Red Hat

"I really enjoyed reading Dan's book. He explains important Python aspects with clear examples (using two twin cats to explain 'is' vs '==' for example).

It is not just code samples, it discusses relevant implementation details comprehensibly. What really matters though is that this book makes you write better Python code!

The book is actually responsible for recent new good Python habits I picked up, for example: using custom exceptions and ABC's (I found Dan's blog searching for abstract classes.) These new learnings alone are worth the price."

— **Bob Belderbos**, Engineer at Oracle & Co-Founder of PyBites

Contents

Contents

Foreword

It's been almost ten years since I first got acquainted with Python as a programming language. When I first learned Python many years ago, it was with a little reluctance. I had been programming in a different language before, and all of the sudden at work, I was assigned to a different team where everyone used Python. That was the beginning of my own Python journey.

When I was first introduced to Python, I was told that it was going to be easy, that I should be able to pick it up quickly. When I asked my colleagues for resources for learning Python, all they gave me was a link to Python's official documentation. Reading the documentation was confusing at first, and it really took me a while before I even felt comfortable navigating through it. Often I found myself needing to look for answers in StackOverflow.

Coming from a different programming language, I wasn't looking for just any resource for learning how to program or what classes and objects are. I was looking for specific resources that would teach me the features of Python, what sets it apart, and how writing in Python is different than writing code in another language.

It really has taken me many years to fully appreciate this language. As I read Dan's book, I kept thinking that I wished I had access to a book like this when I started learning Python many years ago.

For example, one of the many unique Python features that surprised me at first were list comprehensions. As Dan mentions in the book, a tell of someone who just came to Python from a different language is the way they use for-loops. I recall one of the earliest code review comments I got when I started programming in Python was, "Why not use list comprehension here?" Dan explains this concept clearly in section 6, starting by showing how to loop the Pythonic way and building it all the way up to iterators and generators.

In chapter 2.5, Dan discusses the different ways to do string formatting in Python. String formatting is one of those things that defy the Zen of Python, that there should only be one obvious way to do things. Dan shows us the different ways, including my favorite new addition to the language, the f-strings, and he also explains the pros and cons of each method.

The Pythonic Productivity Techniques section is another great resource. It covers aspects beyond the Python programming language, and also includes tips on how to debug your programs, how to manage the dependencies, and gives you a peek inside Python bytecode.

It truly is an honor and my pleasure to introduce this book, Python Tricks, by my friend, Dan Bader.

By contributing to Python as a CPython core developer, I get connected to many members of the community. In my journey, I found mentors, allies, and made many new friends. They remind me that Python is not just about the code, Python is a community.

Mastering Python programming isn't just about grasping the theoretical aspects of the language. It's just as much about understanding and adopting the conventions and best practices used by its community.

Dan's book will help you on this journey. I'm convinced that you'll be more confident when writing Python programs after reading it.

— **Mariatta Wijaya**, Python Core Developer (mariatta.ca)

Chapter 1

Introduction

1.1   What's a Python Trick?

> **Python Trick**: *A short Python code snippet meant as a teaching tool. A Python Trick either teaches an aspect of Python with a simple illustration, or it serves as a motivating example, enabling you to dig deeper and develop an intuitive understanding.*

Python Tricks started out as a short series of code screenshots that I shared on Twitter for a week. To my surprise, they got rave responses and were shared and retweeted for days on end.

More and more developers started asking me for a way to "get the whole series." Actually, I only had a few of these tricks lined up, spanning a variety of Python-related topics. There wasn't a master plan behind them. They were just a fun little Twitter experiment.

But from these inquiries I got the sense that my short-and-sweet code examples would be worth exploring as a teaching tool. Eventually I set out to create a few more Python Tricks and shared them in an email series. Within a few days, several hundred Python developers had signed up and I was just blown away by that response.

Over the following days and weeks, a steady stream of Python developers reached out to me. They thanked me for making a part of the language they were struggling to understand *click* for them. Hearing this feedback felt awesome. I thought these Python Tricks were just code screenshots, but so many developers were getting a lot of value out of them.

That's when I decided to double down on my Python Tricks experiment and expanded it into a series of around 30 emails. Each of these was still just a a headline and a code screenshot, and I soon realized the limits of that format. Around this time, a blind Python developer emailed me, disappointed to find that these Python Tricks were delivered as images he couldn't read with his screen reader.

Clearly, I needed to invest more time into this project to make it more appealing and more accessible to a wider audience. So, I sat down to re-create the whole series of Python Tricks emails in plain text and with proper HTML-based syntax highlighting. That new iteration of Python Tricks chugged along nicely for a while. Based on the responses I got, developers seemed happy they could finally copy and paste the code samples in order to play around with them.

As more and more developers signed up for the email series, I started noticing a pattern in the replies and questions I received. Some Tricks worked well as motivational examples by themselves. However, for the more complex ones there was no narrator to guide readers or to give them additional resources to develop a deeper understanding.

Let's just say this was another big area of improvement. My mission statement for dbader.org is to *help Python developers become more awesome*—and this was clearly an opportunity to get closer to that goal.

I decided to take the best and most valuable Python Tricks from the email course, and I started writing a new kind of Python book around them:

- A book that teaches the coolest aspects of the language with short and easy-to-digest examples.
- A book that works like a buffet of awesome Python features (yum!) and keeps motivation levels high.
- A book that takes you by the hand to guide you and help you deepen your understanding of Python.

This book is really a labor of love for me and also a huge experiment. I hope you'll enjoy reading it and learn something about Python in the process!

— Dan Bader

1.2 What This Book Will Do for You

My goal for this book is to make you a better—more effective, more knowledgeable, more practical—Python developer. You might be wondering, *How will reading this book help me achieve all that?*

Python Tricks is not a step-by-step Python tutorial. It is not an entry-level Python course. If you're in the beginning stages of learning Python, the book alone won't transform you into a professional Python developer. Reading it will still be beneficial to you, but you need to make sure you're working with some other resources to build up your foundational Python skills.

You'll get the most out of this book if you already have some knowledge of Python, and you want to get to the next level. It will work great for you if you've been coding Python for a while and you're ready to go deeper, to round out your knowledge, and to make your code more Pythonic.

Reading *Python Tricks* will also be great for you if you already have experience with other programming languages and you're looking to get up to speed with Python. You'll discover a ton of practical tips and design patterns that'll make you a more effective and skilled Python coder.

1.3 How to Read This Book

The best way to read *Python Tricks: The Book* is to treat it like a buffet of awesome Python features. Each Python Trick in the book is self-contained, so it's completely okay to jump straight to the ones that look the most interesting. In fact, I would encourage you to do just that.

Of course, you can also read through all the Python Tricks in the order they're laid out in the book. That way you won't miss any of them, and you'll know you've seen it all when you arrive at the final page.

Some of these tricks will be easy to understand right away, and you'll have no trouble incorporating them into your day to day work just by reading the chapter. Other tricks might require a bit more time to crack.

If you're having trouble making a particular trick work in your own programs, it helps to play through each of the code examples in a Python interpreter session.

If that doesn't make things click, then please feel free to reach out to me, so I can help you out and improve the explanation in this book. In the long run, that benefits not just you but all Pythonistas reading this book.

1.4 Free Bonus: The Python Tricks Digital Toolkit

This book comes with a collection of bonus resources that I'm calling the Python Tricks Digital Toolkit.

Among other things, the toolkit includes 12 HD-quality Python tutorial videos that add up to over two hours of run-length. These video tutorials go hand-in-hand with select chapters in the book to help you learn faster and retain your knowledge by reinforcing the key points.

I'd value the resources included in this toolkit at $100, but they're included at no extra charge with your purchase of this book.

You can access your copy of the digital toolkit online on my website at dbader.org/python-tricks-toolkit.

Chapter 2

Patterns for Cleaner Python

2.1   Covering Your A** With Assertions

Sometimes a genuinely helpful language feature gets less attention than it deserves. For some reason, this is what happened to Python's built-in `assert` statement.

In this chapter I'm going to give you an introduction to using assertions in Python. You'll learn how to use them to help automatically detect errors in your Python programs. This will make your programs more reliable and easier to debug.

At this point, you might be wondering "What are assertions and what are they good for?" Let's get you some answers for that.

At its core, Python's assert statement is a debugging aid that tests a condition. If the assert condition is true, nothing happens, and your program continues to execute as normal. But if the condition evaluates to false, an `AssertionError` exception is raised with an optional error message.

Assert in Python — An Example

Here's a simple example so you can see where assertions might come in handy. I tried to give this some semblance of a real-world problem you might actually encounter in one of your programs.

Suppose you were building an online store with Python. You're working to add a discount coupon functionality to the system, and eventually you write the following `apply_discount` function:

```python
def apply_discount(product, discount):
    price = int(product['price'] * (1.0 - discount))
    assert 0 <= price <= product['price']
    return price
```

Notice the `assert` statement in there? It will guarantee that, no matter what, discounted prices calculated by this function cannot be lower than $0 and they cannot be higher than the original price of the product.

Let's make sure this actually works as intended if we call this function to apply a valid discount. In this example, products for our store will be represented as plain dictionaries. This is probably not what you'd do for a real application, but it'll work nicely for demonstrating assertions. Let's create an example product—a pair of nice shoes at a price of $149.00:

```
>>> shoes = {'name': 'Fancy Shoes', 'price': 14900}
```

By the way, did you notice how I avoided currency rounding issues by using an integer to represent the price amount in cents? That's generally a good idea... But I digress. Now, if we apply a 25% discount to these shoes, we would expect to arrive at a sale price of $111.75:

```
>>> apply_discount(shoes, 0.25)
11175
```

Alright, this worked nicely. Now, let's try to apply some invalid discounts. For example, a 200% "discount" that would lead to us giving money to the customer:

```
>>> apply_discount(shoes, 2.0)
Traceback (most recent call last):
  File "<input>", line 1, in <module>
    apply_discount(prod, 2.0)
  File "<input>", line 4, in apply_discount
    assert 0 <= price <= product['price']
AssertionError
```

As you can see, when we try to apply this invalid discount, our program halts with an AssertionError. This happens because a discount of 200% violated the assertion condition we placed in the apply_discount function.

You can also see how the exception stacktrace points out the exact line of code containing the failed assertion. If you (or another developer on your team) ever encounter one of these errors while testing the online store, it will be easy to find out what happened just by looking at the exception traceback.

This speeds up debugging efforts considerably, and it will make your programs more maintainable in the long-run. And that, my friend, is the power of assertions.

Why Not Just Use a Regular Exception?

Now, you're probably wondering why I didn't just use an if-statement and an exception in the previous example...

You see, the proper use of assertions is to inform developers about *unrecoverable* errors in a program. Assertions are *not* intended to signal expected error conditions, like a File-Not-Found error, where a user can take corrective actions or just try again.

Assertions are meant to be *internal self-checks* for your program. They work by declaring some conditions as *impossible* in your code. If one of these conditions doesn't hold, that means there's a bug in the program.

If your program is bug-free, these conditions will never occur. But if they *do* occur, the program will crash with an assertion error telling you exactly which "impossible" condition was triggered. This makes it much easier to track down and fix bugs in your programs. And I like anything that makes life easier—don't you?

For now, keep in mind that Python's assert statement is a debugging aid, not a mechanism for handling run-time errors. The goal of using assertions is to let developers find the likely root cause of a bug more quickly. An assertion error should never be raised unless there's a bug in your program.

Let's take a closer look at some other things we can do with assertions, and then I'll cover two common pitfalls when using them in real-world scenarios.

Python's Assert Syntax

It's always a good idea to study up on how a language feature is actually implemented in Python before you start using it. So let's take a quick look at the syntax for the assert statement, according to the Python docs:[1]

```
assert_stmt ::= "assert" expression1 ["," expression2]
```

In this case, expression1 is the condition we test, and the optional expression2 is an error message that's displayed if the assertion fails. At execution time, the Python interpreter transforms each assert statement into roughly the following sequence of statements:

```
if __debug__:
    if not expression1:
        raise AssertionError(expression2)
```

Two interesting things about this code snippet:

Before the assert condition is checked, there's an additional check for the __debug__ global variable. It's a built-in boolean flag that's true under normal circumstances and false if optimizations are requested. We'll talk some more about later that in the "common pitfalls" section.

Also, you can use expression2 to pass an optional error message that will be displayed with the AssertionError in the traceback. This can simplify debugging even further. For example, I've seen code like this:

```
>>> if cond == 'x':
...     do_x()
```

---

[1]cf. Python Docs: "The Assert Statement"

```
... elif cond == 'y':
...     do_y()
... else:
...     assert False, (
...         'This should never happen, but it does '
...         'occasionally. We are currently trying to '
...         'figure out why. Email dbader if you '
...         'encounter this in the wild. Thanks!')
```

Is this ugly? Well, yes. But it's definitely a valid and helpful technique if you're faced with a Heisenbug[2] in one of your applications.

Common Pitfalls With Using Asserts in Python

Before you move on, there are two important caveats regarding the use of assertions in Python that I'd like to call out.

The first one has to do with introducing security risks and bugs into your applications, and the second one is about a syntax quirk that makes it easy to write *useless* assertions.

This sounds (and potentially is) quite horrible, so you should probably at least skim these two caveats below.

Caveat #1 – Don't Use Asserts for Data Validation

The biggest caveat with using asserts in Python is that assertions can be globally disabled[3] with the -O and -OO command line switches, as well as the PYTHONOPTIMIZE environment variable in CPython.

This turns any assert statement into a null-operation: the assertions simply get compiled away and won't be evaluated, which means that none of the conditional expressions will be executed.

---

[2] cf. Wikipedia: Heisenbug
[3] cf. Python Docs: "Constants (__debug__)"

This is an intentional design decision used similarly by many other programming languages. As a side-effect, it becomes extremely dangerous to use assert statements as a quick and easy way to validate input data.

Let me explain—if your program uses asserts to check if a function argument contains a "wrong" or unexpected value, this can backfire quickly and lead to bugs or security holes.

Let's take a look at a simple example that demonstrates this problem. Again, imagine you're building an online store application with Python. Somewhere in your application code there's a function to delete a product as per a user's request.

Because you just learned about assertions, you're eager to use them in your code (hey, I know I would be!) and you write the following implementation:

```python
def delete_product(prod_id, user):
    assert user.is_admin(), 'Must be admin'
    assert store.has_product(prod_id), 'Unknown product'
    store.get_product(prod_id).delete()
```

Take a close look at this `delete_product` function. Now, what's going to happen if assertions are disabled?

There are two serious issues in this three-line function example, and they're caused by the incorrect use of assert statements:

1. **Checking for admin privileges with an assert statement is dangerous.** If assertions are disabled in the Python interpreter, this turns into a null-op. Therefore *any user can now delete products*. The privileges check doesn't even run. This likely introduces a security problem and opens the door for attackers to destroy or severely damage the data in our online store. Not good.

2. **The `has_product()` check is skipped when assertions are disabled.** This means `get_product()` can now be called with invalid product IDs—which could lead to more severe bugs, depending on how our program is written. In the worst case, this could be an avenue for someone to launch Denial of Service attacks against our store. For example, if the store app crashes if someone attempts to delete an unknown product, an attacker could bombard it with invalid delete requests and cause an outage.

How might we avoid these problems? The answer is to *never* use assertions to do data validation. Instead, we could do our validation with regular `if`-statements and raise validation exceptions if necessary, like so:

```python
def delete_product(product_id, user):
    if not user.is_admin():
        raise AuthError('Must be admin to delete')
    if not store.has_product(product_id):
        raise ValueError('Unknown product id')
    store.get_product(product_id).delete()
```

This updated example also has the benefit that instead of raising unspecific `AssertionError` exceptions, it now raises semantically correct exceptions like `ValueError` or `AuthError` (which we'd have to define ourselves.)

Caveat #2 – Asserts That Never Fail

It's surprisingly easy to accidentally write Python assert statements that always evaluate to true. I've been bitten by this myself in the past. Here's the problem, in a nutshell:

When you pass a tuple as the first argument in an `assert` statement, the assertion always evaluates as true and therefore never fails.

For example, this assertion will never fail:

```
assert(1 == 2, 'This should fail')
```

This has to do with non-empty tuples always being truthy in Python. If you pass a tuple to an assert statement, it leads to the assert condition always being true—which in turn leads to the above assert statement being *useless* because it can never fail and trigger an exception.

It's relatively easy to accidentally write bad multi-line asserts due to this, well, unintuitive behavior. For example, I merrily wrote a bunch of broken test cases that gave a false sense of security in one of my test suites. Imagine you had this assertion in one of your unit tests:

```
assert (
    counter == 10,
    'It should have counted all the items'
)
```

Upon first inspection, this test case looks completely fine. However, it would never catch an incorrect result: the assertion always evaluates to True, regardless of the state of the counter variable. And why is that? Because it asserts the truth value of a tuple object.

Like I said, it's rather easy to shoot yourself in the foot with this (mine still hurts). A good countermeasure you can apply to prevent this syntax quirk from causing trouble is to use a code linter.[4] Newer versions of Python 3 will also show a syntax warning for these dubious asserts.

By the way, that's also why you should always do a quick smoke test with your unit test cases. Make sure they can actually fail before you move on to writing the next one.

---

[4]I wrote an article about avoiding bogus assertions in your Python tests. You can find it here: dbader.org/blog/catching-bogus-python-asserts.

Python Assertions — Summary

Despite these caveats I believe that Python's assertions are a powerful debugging tool that's frequently underused by Python developers.

Understanding how assertions work and when to apply them can help you write Python programs that are more maintainable and easier to debug.

It's a great skill to learn that will help bring your Python knowledge to the next level and make you a more well-rounded Pythonista. I know it has saved me hours upon hours of debugging.

Key Takeaways

- Python's assert statement is a debugging aid that tests a condition as an internal self-check in your program.
- Asserts should only be used to help developers identify bugs. They're not a mechanism for handling run-time errors.
- Asserts can be globally disabled with an interpreter setting.

2.2 Complacent Comma Placement

Here's a handy tip for when you're adding and removing items from a list, dict, or set constant in Python: Just end all of your lines with a comma.

Not sure what I'm talking about? Let me give you a quick example. Imagine you've got this list of names in your code:

```
>>> names = ['Alice', 'Bob', 'Dilbert']
```

Whenever you make a change to this list of names, it'll be hard to tell what was modified by looking at a Git diff, for example. Most source control systems are line-based and have a hard time highlighting multiple changes to a single line.

A quick fix for that is to adopt a code style where you spread out list, dict, or set constants across multiple lines, like so:

```
>>> names = [
...     'Alice',
...     'Bob',
...     'Dilbert'
... ]
```

That way there's one item per line, making it perfectly clear which one was added, removed, or modified when you view a diff in your source control system. It's a small change but I found it helped me avoid silly mistakes. It also made it easier for my teammates to review my code changes.

Now, there are two editing cases that can still cause some confusion. Whenever you add a new item at the end of a list, or you remove the last item, you'll have to update the comma placement manually to get consistent formatting.

Let's say you'd like to add another name (*Jane*) to that list. If you add *Jane*, you'll need to fix the comma placement after the *Dilbert* line to avoid a nasty error:

```
>>> names = [
...       'Alice',
...       'Bob',
...       'Dilbert'  # <- Missing comma!
...       'Jane'
]
```

When you inspect the contents of that list, brace yourself for a surprise:

```
>>> names
['Alice', 'Bob', 'DilbertJane']
```

As you can see, Python *merged* the strings *Dilbert* and *Jane* into *DilbertJane*. This so-called "string literal concatenation" is intentional and documented behavior. And it's also a fantastic way to shoot yourself in the foot by introducing hard-to-catch bugs into your programs:

> "Multiple adjacent string or bytes literals (delimited by whitespace), possibly using different quoting conventions, are allowed, and their meaning is the same as their concatenation."[5]

Still, string literal concatenation is a useful feature in some cases. For example, you can use it to reduce the number of backslashes needed to split long string constants across multiple lines:

---

[5]cf. Python Docs: "String literal concatenation"

```
my_str = ('This is a super long string constant '
          'spread out across multiple lines. '
          'And look, no backslash characters needed!')
```

On the other hand, we've just seen how the same feature can quickly turn into a liability. Now, how do we fix this situation?

Adding the missing comma after *Dilbert* prevents the two strings from getting merged into one:

```
>>> names = [
...      'Alice',
...      'Bob',
...      'Dilbert',
...      'Jane'
]
```

But now we've come full circle and returned to the original problem. I had to modify two lines in order to add a new name to the list. This makes it harder to see what was modified in the Git diff again... Did someone add a new name? Did someone change Dilbert's name?

Luckily, Python's syntax allows for some leeway to solve this comma placement issue once and for all. You just need to train yourself to adopt a code style that avoids it in the first place. Let me show you how.

In Python, you can place a comma after every item in a list, dict, or set constant, including the last item. That way, you can just remember to always end your lines with a comma and thus avoid the comma placement juggling that would otherwise be required.

Here's what the final example looks like:

```
>>> names = [
...      'Alice',
```

```
...         'Bob',
...         'Dilbert',
... ]
```

Did you spot the comma after *Dilbert*? That'll make it easy to add or remove new items without having to update the comma placement. It keeps your lines consistent, your source control diffs clean, and your code reviewers happy. Hey, sometimes the magic is in the little things, right?

Key Takeaways

- Smart formatting and comma placement can make your list, dict, or set constants easier to maintain.
- Python's string literal concatenation feature can work to your benefit, or introduce hard-to-catch bugs.

2.3 Context Managers and the with Statement

The with statement in Python is regarded as an obscure feature by some. But when you peek behind the scenes, you'll see that there's no *magic* involved, and it's actually a highly useful feature that can help you write cleaner and more readable Python code.

So what's the with statement good for? It helps simplify some common resource management patterns by abstracting their functionality and allowing them to be factored out and reused.

A good way to see this feature used effectively is by looking at examples in the Python standard library. The built-in open() function provides us with an excellent use case:

```python
with open('hello.txt', 'w') as f:
    f.write('hello, world!')
```

Opening files using the with statement is generally recommended because it ensures that open file descriptors are closed automatically after program execution leaves the context of the with statement. Internally, the above code sample translates to something like this:

```python
f = open('hello.txt', 'w')
try:
    f.write('hello, world')
finally:
    f.close()
```

You can already tell that this is quite a bit more verbose. Note that the try...finally statement is significant. It wouldn't be enough to just write something like this:

```python
f = open('hello.txt', 'w')
f.write('hello, world')
f.close()
```

This implementation won't guarantee the file is closed if there's an exception during the f.write() call—and therefore our program might leak a file descriptor. That's why the with statement is so useful. It makes properly acquiring and releasing resources a breeze.

Another good example where the with statement is used effectively in the Python standard library is the threading.Lock class:

```python
some_lock = threading.Lock()

# Harmful:
some_lock.acquire()
try:
    # Do something...
finally:
    some_lock.release()

# Better:
with some_lock:
    # Do something...
```

In both cases, using a with statement allows you to abstract away most of the resource handling logic. Instead of having to write an explicit try...finally statement each time, using the with statement takes care of that for us.

The with statement can make code that deals with system resources more readable. It also helps you avoid bugs or leaks by making it practically impossible to forget to clean up or release a resource when it's no longer needed.

Supporting with in Your Own Objects

Now, there's nothing special or magical about the open() function or the threading.Lock class and the fact that they can be used with a with statement. You can provide the same functionality in your own classes and functions by implementing so-called *context managers*.[6]

What's a context manager? It's a simple "protocol" (or interface) that your object needs to follow in order to support the with statement. Basically, all you need to do is add __enter__ and __exit__ methods to an object if you want it to function as a context manager. Python will call these two methods at the appropriate times in the resource management cycle.

Let's take a look at what this would look like in practical terms. Here's what a simple implementation of the open() context manager might look like:

```python
class ManagedFile:
    def __init__(self, name):
        self.name = name

    def __enter__(self):
        self.file = open(self.name, 'w')
        return self.file

    def __exit__(self, exc_type, exc_val, exc_tb):
        if self.file:
            self.file.close()
```

Our ManagedFile class follows the context manager protocol and now supports the with statement, just like the original open() example did:

---

[6]cf. Python Docs: "With Statement Context Managers"

```
>>> with ManagedFile('hello.txt') as f:
...     f.write('hello, world!')
...     f.write('bye now')
```

Python calls __enter__ when execution *enters* the context of the with statement and it's time to acquire the resource. When execution *leaves* the context again, Python calls __exit__ to free up the resource.

Writing a class-based context manager isn't the only way to support the with statement in Python. The contextlib[7] utility module in the standard library provides a few more abstractions built on top of the basic context manager protocol. This can make your life a little easier if your use cases match what's offered by contextlib.

For example, you can use the contextlib.contextmanager decorator to define a generator-based *factory function* for a resource that will then automatically support the with statement. Here's what rewriting our ManagedFile context manager example with this technique looks like:

```
from contextlib import contextmanager

@contextmanager
def managed_file(name):
    try:
        f = open(name, 'w')
        yield f
    finally:
        f.close()

>>> with managed_file('hello.txt') as f:
...     f.write('hello, world!')
...     f.write('bye now')
```

---

[7]cf. Python Docs: "contextlib"

In this case, `managed_file()` is a generator that first acquires the resource. After that, it temporarily suspends its own execution and *yields* the resource so it can be used by the caller. When the caller leaves the `with` context, the generator continues to execute so that any remaining clean-up steps can occur and the resource can get released back to the system.

The class-based implementation and the generator-based one are essentially equivalent. You might prefer one over the other, depending on which approach you find more readable.

A downside of the `@contextmanager`-based implementation might be that it requires some understanding of advanced Python concepts like decorators and generators. If you need to get up to speed with those, feel free to take a detour to the relevant chapters here in this book.

Once again, making the right implementation choice here comes down to what you and your team are comfortable using and what you find the most readable.

Writing Pretty APIs With Context Managers

Context managers are quite flexible, and if you use the `with` statement creatively, you can define convenient APIs for your modules and classes.

For example, what if the "resource" we wanted to manage was text indentation levels in some kind of report generator program? What if we could write code like this to do it:

```
with Indenter() as indent:
    indent.print('hi!')
    with indent:
        indent.print('hello')
        with indent:
            indent.print('bonjour')
    indent.print('hey')
```

This almost reads like a domain-specific language (DSL) for indent-
ing text. Also, notice how this code enters and leaves the same context manager multiple times to change indentation levels. Running
this code snippet should lead to the following output and print neatly
formatted text to the console:

```
hi!
    hello
        bonjour
hey
```

So, how would you implement a context manager to support this functionality?

By the way, this could be a great exercise for you to understand exactly
how context managers work. So before you check out my implementation below, you might want to take some time and try to implement
this yourself as a learning exercise.

If you're ready to check out my implementation, here's how you might
implement this functionality using a class-based context manager:

```python
class Indenter:
    def __init__(self):
        self.level = 0

    def __enter__(self):
        self.level += 1
        return self

    def __exit__(self, exc_type, exc_val, exc_tb):
        self.level -= 1

    def print(self, text):
        print('    ' * self.level + text)
```

That wasn't so bad, was it? I hope that by now you're already feeling more comfortable using context managers and the with statement in your own Python programs. They're an excellent feature that will allow you to deal with resource management in a much more Pythonic and maintainable way.

If you're looking for another exercise to deepen your understanding, try implementing a context manager that measures the execution time of a code block using the time.time function. Be sure to try out writing both a decorator-based and a class-based variant to drive home the difference between the two.

Key Takeaways

- The with statement simplifies exception handling by encapsulating standard uses of try/finally statements in so-called context managers.
- Most commonly it is used to manage the safe acquisition and release of system resources. Resources are acquired by the with statement and released automatically when execution leaves the with context.
- Using with effectively can help you avoid resource leaks and make your code easier to read.

2.4   Underscores, Dunders, and More

Single and double underscores have a meaning in Python variable and method names. Some of that meaning is merely by convention and intended as a hint to the programmer—and some of it is enforced by the Python interpreter.

If you're wondering, *"What's the meaning of single and double under-scores in Python variable and method names?"* I'll do my best to get you the answer here. In this chapter we'll discuss the following five underscore patterns and naming conventions, and how they affect the behavior of your Python programs:

- Single Leading Underscore: _var
- Single Trailing Underscore: var_
- Double Leading Underscore: __var
- Double Leading and Trailing Underscore: __var__
- Single Underscore: _

1. Single Leading Underscore: "_var"

When it comes to variable and method names, the single under-score prefix has a meaning by convention only. It's a hint to the programmer—it means what the Python community agrees it should mean, but it does not affect the behavior of your programs.

The underscore prefix is meant as a *hint* to tell another programmer that a variable or method starting with a single underscore is intended for internal use. This convention is defined in PEP 8, the most commonly used Python code style guide.[8]

However, this convention isn't enforced by the Python interpreter. Python does not have strong distinctions between "private" and "public" variables like Java does. Adding a single underscore in front of a variable name is more like someone putting up a tiny underscore

---

[8]cf. PEP 8: "Style Guide for Python Code"

warning sign that says: *"Hey, this isn't really meant to be a part of the public interface of this class. Best to leave it alone."*

Take a look at the following example:

```python
class Test:
    def __init__(self):
        self.foo = 11
        self._bar = 23
```

What's going to happen if you instantiate this class and try to access the foo and _bar attributes defined in its __init__ constructor?

Let's find out:

```python
>>> t = Test()
>>> t.foo
11
>>> t._bar
23
```

As you can see, the leading single underscore in _bar did not prevent us from "reaching into" the class and accessing the value of that variable.

That's because the single underscore prefix in Python is merely an agreed-upon convention—at least when it comes to variable and method names. However, leading underscores do impact how names get imported from modules. Imagine you had the following code in a module called my_module:

```python
# my_module.py:

def external_func():
    return 23
```

```
def _internal_func():
    return 42
```

Now, if you use a *wildcard import* to import all the names from the module, Python will *not* import names with a leading underscore (unless the module defines an __all__ list that overrides this behavior[9]):

```
>>> from my_module import *
>>> external_func()
23
>>> _internal_func()
NameError: "name '_internal_func' is not defined"
```

By the way, wildcard imports should be avoided as they make it unclear which names are present in the namespace.[10] It's better to stick to regular imports for the sake of clarity. Unlike wildcard imports, regular imports are not affected by the leading single underscore naming convention:

```
>>> import my_module
>>> my_module.external_func()
23
>>> my_module._internal_func()
42
```

I know this might be a little confusing at this point. If you stick to the PEP 8 recommendation that wildcard imports should be avoided, then all you really need to remember is this:

Single underscores are a Python naming convention that indicates a name is meant for internal use. It is generally not enforced by the Python interpreter and is only meant as a hint to the programmer.

---

[9] cf. Python Docs: "Importing * From a Package"
[10] cf. PEP 8: "Imports"

2. Single Trailing Underscore: "var_"

Sometimes the most fitting name for a variable is already taken by a keyword in the Python language. Therefore, names like class or def cannot be used as variable names in Python. In this case, you can append a single underscore to break the naming conflict:

```
>>> def make_object(name, class):
SyntaxError: "invalid syntax"

>>> def make_object(name, class_):
...     pass
```

In summary, a single trailing underscore (postfix) is used by convention to avoid naming conflicts with Python keywords. This convention is defined and explained in PEP 8.

3. Double Leading Underscore: "__var"

The naming patterns we've covered so far receive their meaning from agreed-upon conventions only. With Python class attributes (variables and methods) that start with double underscores, things are a little different.

A double underscore prefix causes the Python interpreter to rewrite the attribute name in order to avoid naming conflicts in subclasses.

This is also called *name mangling*—the interpreter changes the name of the variable in a way that makes it harder to create collisions when the class is extended later.

I know this sounds rather abstract. That's why I put together this little code example we can use for experimentation:

```
class Test:
    def __init__(self):
        self.foo = 11
```

```
        self._bar = 23
        self.__baz = 42
```

Let's take a look at the attributes on this object using the built-in dir() function:

```
>>> t = Test()
>>> dir(t)
['_Test__baz', '__class__', '__delattr__', '__dict__',
  '__dir__', '__doc__', '__eq__', '__format__', '__ge__',
  '__getattribute__', '__gt__', '__hash__', '__init__',
  '__le__', '__lt__', '__module__', '__ne__', '__new__',
  '__reduce__', '__reduce_ex__', '__repr__',
  '__setattr__', '__sizeof__', '__str__',
  '__subclasshook__', '__weakref__', '_bar', 'foo']
```

This gives us a list with the object's attributes. Let's take this list and look for our original variable names foo, _bar, and __baz. I promise you'll notice some interesting changes.

First of all, the self.foo variable appears unmodified as foo in the attribute list.

Next up, self._bar behaves the same way—it shows up on the class as _bar. Like I said before, the leading underscore is just a *convention* in this case—a hint for the programmer.

However, with self.__baz things look a little different. When you search for __baz in that list, you'll see that there is no variable with that name.

So what happened to __baz?

If you look closely, you'll see there's an attribute called _Test__baz on this object. This is the *name mangling* that the Python interpreter applies. It does this to protect the variable from getting overridden in subclasses.

Let's create another class that extends the Test class and attempts to override its existing attributes added in the constructor:

```
class ExtendedTest(Test):
    def __init__(self):
        super().__init__()
        self.foo = 'overridden'
        self._bar = 'overridden'
        self.__baz = 'overridden'
```

Now, what do you think the values of foo, _bar, and __baz will be on instances of this ExtendedTest class? Let's take a look:

```
>>> t2 = ExtendedTest()
>>> t2.foo
'overridden'
>>> t2._bar
'overridden'
>>> t2.__baz
AttributeError:
"'ExtendedTest' object has no attribute '__baz'"
```

Wait, why did we get that AttributeError when we tried to inspect the value of t2.__baz? Name mangling strikes again! It turns out this object doesn't even have a __baz attribute:

```
>>> dir(t2)
['_ExtendedTest__baz', '_Test__baz', '__class__',
 '__delattr__', '__dict__', '__dir__', '__doc__',
 '__eq__', '__format__', '__ge__', '__getattribute__',
 '__gt__', '__hash__', '__init__', '__le__', '__lt__',
 '__module__', '__ne__', '__new__', '__reduce__',
 '__reduce_ex__', '__repr__', '__setattr__',
 '__sizeof__', '__str__', '__subclasshook__',
 '__weakref__', '_bar', 'foo', 'get_vars']
```

As you can see, __baz got turned into _ExtendedTest__baz to prevent accidental modification. But the original _Test__baz is also still around:

```
>>> t2._ExtendedTest__baz
'overridden'
>>> t2._Test__baz
42
```

Double underscore name mangling is fully transparent to the programmer. Take a look at the following example that will confirm this:

```
class ManglingTest:
    def __init__(self):
        self.__mangled = 'hello'

    def get_mangled(self):
        return self.__mangled

>>> ManglingTest().get_mangled()
'hello'
>>> ManglingTest().__mangled
AttributeError:
"'ManglingTest' object has no attribute '__mangled'"
```

Does name mangling also apply to method names? It sure does! Name mangling affects *all* names that start with two underscore characters ("dunders") in a class context:

```
class MangledMethod:
    def __method(self):
        return 42

    def call_it(self):
```

```
      return self.__method()

>>> MangledMethod().__method()
AttributeError:
"'MangledMethod' object has no attribute '__method'"
>>> MangledMethod().call_it()
42
```

Here's another, perhaps surprising, example of name mangling in action:

```
_MangledGlobal__mangled = 23

class MangledGlobal:
    def test(self):
        return __mangled

>>> MangledGlobal().test()
23
```

In this example, I declared _MangledGlobal__mangled as a global variable. Then I accessed the variable inside the context of a class named MangledGlobal. Because of name mangling, I was able to reference the _MangledGlobal__mangled global variable as just __mangled inside the test() method on the class.

The Python interpreter automatically expanded the name __mangled to _MangledGlobal__mangled because it begins with two underscore characters. This demonstrates that name mangling isn't tied to class attributes specifically. It applies to any name starting with two underscore characters that is used in a class context.

Whew! That was a lot to absorb.

To be honest with you, I didn't write down these examples and explanations off the top of my head. It took me some research and editing to do it. I've been using Python for years but rules and special cases like that aren't constantly on my mind.

Sometimes the most important skills for a programmer are "pattern recognition" and knowing where to look things up. If you feel a little overwhelmed at this point, don't worry. Take your time and play with some of the examples in this chapter.

Let these concepts sink in enough so that you'll recognize the general idea of name mangling and some of the other behaviors I've shown you. If you encounter them "in the wild" one day, you'll know what to look for in the documentation.

Sidebar: What are *dunders*?

If you've heard some experienced Pythonistas talk about Python or watched a few conference talks you may have heard the term *dunder*. If you're wondering what that is, well, here's your answer:

Double underscores are often referred to as "dunders" in the Python community. The reason is that double underscores appear quite often in Python code, and to avoid fatiguing their jaw muscles, Pythonistas often shorten "double underscore" to "dunder."

For example, you'd pronounce __baz as "dunder baz." Likewise, __init__ would be pronounced as "dunder init," even though one might think it should be "dunder init dunder."

But that's just yet another quirk in the naming convention. It's like a *secret handshake* for Python developers.

4. Double Leading and Trailing Underscore: "__var__"

Perhaps surprisingly, name mangling is *not* applied if a name *starts and ends* with double underscores. Variables surrounded by a double underscore prefix and postfix are left unscathed by the Python interpreter:

```
class PrefixPostfixTest:
    def __init__(self):
        self.__bam__ = 42

>>> PrefixPostfixTest().__bam__
42
```

However, names that have both leading and trailing double underscores are reserved for special use in the language. This rule covers things like __init__ for object constructors, or __call__ to make objects callable.

These *dunder methods* are often referred to as *magic methods*—but many people in the Python community, including myself, don't like that word. It implies that the use of dunder methods is discouraged, which is entirely not the case. They're a core feature in Python and should be used as needed. There's nothing "magical" or arcane about them.

However, as far as naming conventions go, it's best to stay away from using names that start and end with double underscores in your own programs to avoid collisions with future changes to the Python language.

5. Single Underscore: "_"

Per convention, a single stand-alone underscore is sometimes used as a name to indicate that a variable is temporary or insignificant.

For example, in the following loop we don't need access to the running index and we can use "_" to indicate that it is just a temporary value:

```
>>> for _ in range(32):
...     print('Hello, World.')
```

You can also use single underscores in unpacking expressions as a "don't care" variable to ignore particular values. Again, this meaning is per convention only and it doesn't trigger any special behaviors in the Python parser. The single underscore is simply a valid variable name that's sometimes used for this purpose.

In the following code example, I'm unpacking a tuple into separate variables but I'm only interested in the values for the color and mileage fields. However, in order for the unpacking expression to succeed, I need to assign all values contained in the tuple to variables. That's where "_" is useful as a placeholder variable:

```
>>> car = ('red', 'auto', 12, 3812.4)
>>> color, _, _, mileage = car

>>> color
'red'
>>> mileage
3812.4
>>> _
12
```

Besides its use as a temporary variable, "_" is a special variable in most Python REPLs that represents the result of the last expression evaluated by the interpreter.

This is handy if you're working in an interpreter session and you'd like to access the result of a previous calculation:

```
>>> 20 + 3
23
>>> _
23
>>> print(_)
23
```

It's also handy if you're constructing objects on the fly and want to interact with them without assigning them a name first:

```
>>> list()
[]
>>> _.append(1)
>>> _.append(2)
>>> _.append(3)
>>> _
[1, 2, 3]
```

Key Takeaways

- **Single Leading Underscore** "_var": Naming convention indicating a name is meant for internal use. Generally not enforced by the Python interpreter (except in wildcard imports) and meant as a hint to the programmer only.

- **Single Trailing Underscore** "var_": Used by convention to avoid naming conflicts with Python keywords.

- **Double Leading Underscore** "__var": Triggers name mangling when used in a class context. Enforced by the Python interpreter.

- **Double Leading and Trailing Underscore** "__var__": Indicates special methods defined by the Python language. Avoid this naming scheme for your own attributes.

- **Single Underscore** "_": Sometimes used as a name for temporary or insignificant variables ("don't care"). Also, it represents the result of the last expression in a Python REPL session.

2.5 A Shocking Truth About String Formatting

Remember the Zen of Python and how there should be "one obvious way to do something?" You might scratch your head when you find out that there are *four* major ways to do string formatting in Python.

In this chapter I'll demonstrate how these four string formatting approaches work and what their respective strengths and weaknesses are. I'll also give you my simple "rule of thumb" for how I pick the best general-purpose string formatting approach.

Let's jump right in, as we've got a lot to cover. In order to have a simple toy example for experimentation, let's assume we've got the following variables (or constants, really) to work with:

```
>>> errno = 50159747054
>>> name = 'Bob'
```

And based on these variables we'd like to generate an output string with the following error message:

```
'Hey Bob, there is a 0xbadc0ffee error!'
```

Now, *that* error could really spoil a dev's Monday morning! But we're here to discuss string formatting today. So let's get to work.

#1 – "Old Style" String Formatting

Strings in Python have a unique built-in operation that can be accessed with the %-operator. It's a shortcut that lets you do simple positional formatting very easily. If you've ever worked with a printf-style function in C, you'll instantly recognize how this works. Here's a simple example:

```
>>> 'Hello, %s' % name
'Hello, Bob'
```

I'm using the %s format specifier here to tell Python where to substitute the value of name, represented as a string. This is called "old style" string formatting.

In old style string formatting there are also other format specifiers available that let you control the output string. For example, it's possible to convert numbers to hexadecimal notation or to add whitespace padding to generate nicely formatted tables and reports.[11]

Here, I'm using the %x format specifier to convert an int value to a string and to represent it as a hexadecimal number:

```
>>> '%x' % errno
'badc0ffee'
```

The "old style" string formatting syntax changes slightly if you want to make multiple substitutions in a single string. Because the %-operator only takes one argument, you need to wrap the right-hand side in a tuple, like so:

```
>>> 'Hey %s, there is a 0x%x error!' % (name, errno)
'Hey Bob, there is a 0xbadc0ffee error!'
```

It's also possible to refer to variable substitutions by name in your format string, if you pass a mapping to the %-operator:

```
>>> 'Hey %(name)s, there is a 0x%(errno)x error!' % {
...         "name": name, "errno": errno }
'Hey Bob, there is a 0xbadc0ffee error!'
```

---

[11]cf. Python Docs: "printf-style String Formatting"

This makes your format strings easier to maintain and easier to modify in the future. You don't have to worry about making sure the order you're passing in the values matches up with the order the values are referenced in the format string. Of course, the downside is that this technique requires a little more typing.

I'm sure you've been wondering why this printf-style formatting is called "old style" string formatting. Well, let me tell you. It was technically superseded by "new style" formatting, which we're going to talk about in a minute. But while "old style" formatting has been de-emphasized, it hasn't been deprecated. It is still supported in the latest versions of Python.

#2 – "New Style" String Formatting

Python 3 introduced a new way to do string formatting that was also later back-ported to Python 2.7. This "new style" string formatting gets rid of the %-operator special syntax and makes the syntax for string formatting more regular. Formatting is now handled by calling a format() function on a string object.[12]

You can use the format() function to do simple positional formatting, just like you could with "old style" formatting:

```
>>> 'Hello, {}'.format(name)
'Hello, Bob'
```

Or, you can refer to your variable substitutions by name and use them in any order you want. This is quite a powerful feature as it allows for re-arranging the order of display without changing the arguments passed to the format function:

```
>>> 'Hey {name}, there is a 0x{errno:x} error!'.format(
...         name=name, errno=errno)
'Hey Bob, there is a 0xbadc0ffee error!'
```

---

[12] cf. Python Docs: "str.format()"

This also shows that the syntax to format an int variable as a hexadecimal string has changed. Now we need to pass a *format spec* by adding a ":x" suffix after the variable name.

Overall, the format string syntax has become more powerful without complicating the simpler use cases. It pays off to read up on this *string formatting mini-language* in the Python documentation.[13]

In Python 3, this "new style" string formatting is preferred over %-style formatting. However, starting with Python 3.6 there's an even better way to format your strings. I'll tell you all about it in the next section.

#3 – Literal String Interpolation (Python 3.6+)

Python 3.6 adds yet another way to format strings, called *Formatted String Literals*. This new way of formatting strings lets you use embedded Python expressions inside string constants. Here's a simple example to give you a feel for the feature:

```
>>> f'Hello, {name}!'
'Hello, Bob!'
```

This new formatting syntax is powerful. Because you can embed arbitrary Python expressions, you can even do inline arithmetic with it, like this:

```
>>> a = 5
>>> b = 10
>>> f'Five plus ten is {a + b} and not {2 * (a + b)}.'

'Five plus ten is 15 and not 30.'
```

Behind the scenes, formatted string literals are a Python parser feature that converts f-strings into a series of string constants and expressions. They then get joined up to build the final string.

---

[13]cf. Python Docs: "Format String Syntax"

Imagine we had the following `greet()` function that contains an f-string:

```
>>> def greet(name, question):
...     return f"Hello, {name}! How's it {question}?"
...

>>> greet('Bob', 'going')
"Hello, Bob! How's it going?"
```

When we disassemble the function and inspect what's going on behind the scenes, we can see that the f-string in the function gets transformed into something similar to the following:

```
>>> def greet(name, question):
...     return ("Hello, " + name + "! How's it " +
            question + "?")
```

The real implementation is slightly faster than that because it uses the BUILD_STRING opcode as an optimization.[14] But functionally they're the same:

```
>>> import dis
>>> dis.dis(greet)
  2       0 LOAD_CONST       1 ('Hello, ')
          2 LOAD_FAST        0 (name)
          4 FORMAT_VALUE     0
          6 LOAD_CONST       2 ("! How's it ")
          8 LOAD_FAST        1 (question)
         10 FORMAT_VALUE     0
         12 LOAD_CONST       3 ('?')
         14 BUILD_STRING     5
         16 RETURN_VALUE
```

---

[14]cf. Python 3 bug-tracker issue #27078

String literals also support the existing format string syntax of the `str.format()` method. That allows you to solve the same formatting problems we've discussed in the previous two sections:

```
>>> f"Hey {name}, there's a {errno:#x} error!"
"Hey Bob, there's a 0xbadc0ffee error!"
```

Python's new Formatted String Literals are similar to the JavaScript Template Literals added in ES2015. I think they're quite a nice addition to the language, and I've already started using them in my day-to-day Python 3 work. You can learn more about Formatted String Literals in the official Python documentation.[15]

#4 – Template Strings

One more technique for string formatting in Python is Template Strings. It's a simpler and less powerful mechanism, but in some cases this might be exactly what you're looking for.

Let's take a look at a simple greeting example:

```
>>> from string import Template
>>> t = Template('Hey, $name!')
>>> t.substitute(name=name)
'Hey, Bob!'
```

You see here that we need to import the `Template` class from Python's built-in `string` module. Template strings are not a core language feature but they're supplied by a module in the standard library.

Another difference is that template strings don't allow format specifiers. So in order to get our error string example to work, we need to transform our int error number into a hex-string ourselves:

---

[15]cf. Python Docs: "Formatted string literals"

```
>>> templ_string = 'Hey $name, there is a $error error!'
>>> Template(templ_string).substitute(
...         name=name, error=hex(errno))
'Hey Bob, there is a 0xbadc0ffee error!'
```

That worked great but you're probably wondering when you use template strings in your Python programs. In my opinion, the best use case for template strings is when you're handling format strings generated by users of your program. Due to their reduced complexity, template strings are a safer choice.

The more complex formatting mini-languages of other string formatting techniques might introduce security vulnerabilities to your programs. For example, it's possible for format strings to access arbitrary variables in your program.

That means, if a malicious user can supply a format string they can also potentially leak secret keys and other sensible information! Here's a simple proof of concept of how this attack might be used:

```
>>> SECRET = 'this-is-a-secret'
>>> class Error:
...         def __init__(self):
...             pass
>>> err = Error()
>>> user_input = '{error.__init__.__globals__[SECRET]}'

# Uh-oh...
>>> user_input.format(error=err)
'this-is-a-secret'
```

See how the hypothetical attacker was able to extract our secret string by accessing the __globals__ dictionary from the format string? Scary, huh! Template Strings close this attack vector, and this makes them a safer choice if you're handling format strings generated from user input:

```
>>> user_input = '${error.__init__.__globals__[SECRET]}'
>>> Template(user_input).substitute(error=err)
ValueError:
"Invalid placeholder in string: line 1, col 1"
```

Which String Formatting Method Should I Use?

I totally get that having so much choice for how to format your strings in Python can feel very confusing. This would be a good time to bust out some flowchart infographic...

But I'm not going to do that. Instead, I'll try to boil it down to the simple rule of thumb that I apply when I'm writing Python.

Here we go—you can use this rule of thumb any time you're having difficulty deciding which string formatting method to use, depending on the circumstances:

Dan's Python String Formatting Rule of Thumb:

> *If your format strings are user-supplied, use Template Strings to avoid security issues. Otherwise, use Literal String Interpolation if you're on Python 3.6+, and "New Style" String Formatting if you're not.*

Key Takeaways

- Perhaps surprisingly, there's more than one way to handle string formatting in Python.
- Each method has its individual pros and cons. Your use case will influence which method you should use.
- If you're having trouble deciding which string formatting method to use, try my *String Formatting Rule of Thumb*.

2.6 "The Zen of Python" Easter Egg

I know what follows is a common sight as far as Python books go. But there's really no way around Tim Peters' *Zen of Python*. I've benefited from revisiting it over the years, and I think Tim's words made me a better coder. Hopefully they can do the same for you.

Also, you can tell the *Zen of Python* is a big deal because it's included as an Easter egg in the language. Just enter a Python interpreter session and run the following:

```
>>> import this
```

The Zen of Python, by Tim Peters

Beautiful is better than ugly.
Explicit is better than implicit.
Simple is better than complex.
Complex is better than complicated.
Flat is better than nested.
Sparse is better than dense.
Readability counts.
Special cases aren't special enough to break the rules.
Although practicality beats purity.
Errors should never pass silently.
Unless explicitly silenced.
In the face of ambiguity, refuse the temptation to guess.
There should be one—and preferably only one—obvious way to do it.
Although that way may not be obvious at first unless you're Dutch.
Now is better than never.
Although never is often better than *right* now.
If the implementation is hard to explain, it's a bad idea.
If the implementation is easy to explain, it may be a good idea.
Namespaces are one honking great idea—let's do more of those!

Chapter 3

Effective Functions

3.1 Python's Functions Are First-Class

Python's functions are first-class objects. You can assign them to variables, store them in data structures, pass them as arguments to other functions, and even return them as values from other functions.

Grokking these concepts intuitively will make understanding advanced features in Python like lambdas and decorators much easier. It also puts you on a path towards functional programming techniques.

Over the next few pages I'll guide you through a number of examples to help you develop this intuitive understanding. The examples will build on top of each other, so you might want to read them in sequence and even to try out some of them in a Python interpreter session as you go along.

Wrapping your head around the concepts we'll be discussing here might take a little longer than you'd expect. Don't worry—that's completely normal. I've been there. You might feel like you're banging your head against the wall, and then suddenly things will "click" and fall into place when you're ready.

Throughout this chapter I'll be using this yell function for demonstration purposes. It's a simple toy example with easily recognizable output:

```python
def yell(text):
    return text.upper() + '!'

>>> yell('hello')
'HELLO!'
```

Functions Are Objects

All data in a Python program is represented by objects or relations between objects.[1] Things like strings, lists, modules, and functions are all objects. There's nothing particularly special about functions in Python. They're also just objects.

Because the yell function is an *object* in Python, you can assign it to another variable, just like any other object:

```
>>> bark = yell
```

This line doesn't call the function. It takes the function object referenced by yell and creates a second name, bark, that points to it. You could now also execute the same underlying function object by calling bark:

```
>>> bark('woof')
'WOOF!'
```

Function objects and their names are two separate concerns. Here's more proof: You can delete the function's original name (yell). Since another name (bark) still points to the underlying function, you can still call the function through it:

```
>>> del yell

>>> yell('hello?')
NameError: "name 'yell' is not defined"

>>> bark('hey')
'HEY!'
```

---

[1] cf. Python Docs: "Objects, values and types"

By the way, Python attaches a string identifier to every function at creation time for debugging purposes. You can access this internal identifier with the __name__ attribute:[2]

```
>>> bark.__name__
'yell'
```

Now, while the function's __name__ is still "yell," that doesn't affect how you can access the function object from your code. The name identifier is merely a debugging aid. A *variable pointing to a function* and the *function itself* are really two separate concerns.

Functions Can Be Stored in Data Structures

Since functions are first-class citizens, you can store them in data structures, just like you can with other objects. For example, you can add functions to a list:

```
>>> funcs = [bark, str.lower, str.capitalize]
>>> funcs
[<function yell at 0x10ff96510>,
 <method 'lower' of 'str' objects>,
 <method 'capitalize' of 'str' objects>]
```

Accessing the function objects stored inside the list works like it would with any other type of object:

```
>>> for f in funcs:
...     print(f, f('hey there'))
<function yell at 0x10ff96510> 'HEY THERE!'
<method 'lower' of 'str' objects> 'hey there'
<method 'capitalize' of 'str' objects> 'Hey there'
```

---

[2]Since Python 3.3 there's also __qualname__ which serves a similar purpose and provides a *qualified name* string to disambiguate function and class names (cf. PEP 3155).

You can even call a function object stored in the list without first assigning it to a variable. You can do the lookup and then immediately call the resulting "disembodied" function object within a single expression:

```
>>> funcs[0]('heyho')
'HEYHO!'
```

Functions Can Be Passed to Other Functions

Because functions are objects, you can pass them as arguments to other functions. Here's a greet function that formats a greeting string using the function object passed to it and then prints it:

```
def greet(func):
    greeting = func('Hi, I am a Python program')
    print(greeting)
```

You can influence the resulting greeting by passing in different functions. Here's what happens if you pass the bark function to greet:

```
>>> greet(bark)
'HI, I AM A PYTHON PROGRAM!'
```

Of course, you could also define a new function to generate a different flavor of greeting. For example, the following whisper function might work better if you don't want your Python programs to sound like Optimus Prime:

```
def whisper(text):
    return text.lower() + '...'
```

```
>>> greet(whisper)
'hi, i am a python program...'
```

63

The ability to pass function objects as arguments to other functions is powerful. It allows you to abstract away and pass around *behavior* in your programs. In this example, the greet function stays the same but you can influence its output by passing in different *greeting behaviors*.

Functions that can accept other functions as arguments are also called *higher-order functions*. They are a necessity for the functional programming style.

The classical example for higher-order functions in Python is the built-in map function. It takes a function object and an iterable, and then calls the function on each element in the iterable, yielding the results as it goes along.

Here's how you might format a sequence of greetings all at once by *mapping* the bark function to them:

```
>>> list(map(bark, ['hello', 'hey', 'hi']))
['HELLO!', 'HEY!', 'HI!']
```

As you saw, map went through the entire list and applied the bark function to each element. As a result, we now have a new list object with modified greeting strings.

Functions Can Be Nested

Perhaps surprisingly, Python allows functions to be defined inside other functions. These are often called *nested functions* or *inner functions*. Here's an example:

```
def speak(text):
    def whisper(t):
        return t.lower() + '...'
    return whisper(text)
```

```
>>> speak('Hello, World')
'hello, world...'
```

Now, what's going on here? Every time you call speak, it defines a new inner function whisper and then calls it immediately after. My brain's starting to itch just a little here but, all in all, that's still relatively straightforward stuff.

Here's the kicker though—whisper *does not exist* outside speak:

```
>>> whisper('Yo')
NameError:
"name 'whisper' is not defined"

>>> speak.whisper
AttributeError:
"'function' object has no attribute 'whisper'"
```

But what if you really wanted to access that nested whisper function from outside speak? Well, functions are objects—you can *return* the inner function to the caller of the parent function.

For example, here's a function defining two inner functions. Depending on the argument passed to top-level function, it selects and returns one of the inner functions to the caller:

```
def get_speak_func(volume):
    def whisper(text):
        return text.lower() + '...'
    def yell(text):
        return text.upper() + '!'
    if volume > 0.5:
        return yell
    else:
        return whisper
```

Notice how `get_speak_func` doesn't actually *call* any of its inner functions—it simply selects the appropriate inner function based on the volume argument and then returns the function object:

```
>>> get_speak_func(0.3)
<function get_speak_func.<locals>.whisper at 0x10ae18>

>>> get_speak_func(0.7)
<function get_speak_func.<locals>.yell at 0x1008c8>
```

Of course, you could then go on and call the returned function, either directly or by assigning it to a variable name first:

```
>>> speak_func = get_speak_func(0.7)
>>> speak_func('Hello')
'HELLO!'
```

Let that sink in for a second here... This means not only can functions *accept behaviors* through arguments but they can also *return behaviors*. How cool is that?

You know what, things are starting to get a little loopy here. I'm going to take a quick coffee break before I continue writing (and I suggest you do the same).

Functions Can Capture Local State

You just saw how functions can contain inner functions, and that it's even possible to return these (otherwise hidden) inner functions from the parent function.

Best put on your seat belt now because it's going to get a little crazier still—we're about to enter even deeper functional programming territory. (You had that coffee break, right?)

Not only can functions return other functions, these inner functions can also *capture and carry some of the parent function's state* with them. Well, what does that mean?

I'm going to slightly rewrite the previous get_speak_func example to illustrate this. The new version takes a "volume" *and* a "text" argument right away to make the returned function immediately callable:

```python
def get_speak_func(text, volume):
    def whisper():
        return text.lower() + '...'
    def yell():
        return text.upper() + '!'
    if volume > 0.5:
        return yell
    else:
        return whisper
```

```python
>>> get_speak_func('Hello, World', 0.7)()
'HELLO, WORLD!'
```

Take a good look at the inner functions whisper and yell now. Notice how they no longer have a text parameter? But somehow they can still access the text parameter defined in the parent function. In fact, they seem to *capture* and "remember" the value of that argument.

Functions that do this are called *lexical closures* (or just *closures*, for short). A closure remembers the values from its enclosing lexical scope even when the program flow is no longer in that scope.

In practical terms, this means not only can functions *return behaviors* but they can also *pre-configure those behaviors*. Here's another barebones example to illustrate this idea:

```python
def make_adder(n):
    def add(x):
        return x + n
```

```
    return add
>>> plus_3 = make_adder(3)
>>> plus_5 = make_adder(5)

>>> plus_3(4)
7
>>> plus_5(4)
9
```

In this example, make_adder serves as a *factory* to create and config-
ure "adder" functions. Notice how the "adder" functions can still access the n argument of the make_adder function (the enclosing scope).

Objects Can Behave Like Functions

While all functions are objects in Python, the reverse isn't true. Objects aren't functions. But they can be made *callable*, which allows
you to *treat them like functions* in many cases.

If an object is callable it means you can use the round parentheses
function call syntax on it and even pass in function call arguments.
This is all powered by the __call__ dunder method. Here's an example of class defining a callable object:

```
class Adder:
    def __init__(self, n):
        self.n = n

    def __call__(self, x):
        return self.n + x

>>> plus_3 = Adder(3)
>>> plus_3(4)
7
```

Behind the scenes, "calling" an object instance as a function attempts to execute the object's __call__ method.

Of course, not all objects will be callable. That's why there's a built-in callable function to check whether an object appears to be callable or not:

```
>>> callable(plus_3)
True
>>> callable(yell)
True
>>> callable('hello')
False
```

Key Takeaways

- Everything in Python is an object, including functions. You can assign them to variables, store them in data structures, and pass or return them to and from other functions (first-class functions.)
- First-class functions allow you to abstract away and pass around behavior in your programs.
- Functions can be nested and they can capture and carry some of the parent function's state with them. Functions that do this are called closures.
- Objects can be made callable. In many cases this allows you to treat them like functions.

3.2 Lambdas Are Single-Expression Functions

The lambda keyword in Python provides a shortcut for declaring small anonymous functions. Lambda functions behave just like regular functions declared with the def keyword. They can be used whenever function objects are required.

For example, this is how you'd define a simple lambda function carrying out an addition:

```
>>> add = lambda x, y: x + y
>>> add(5, 3)
8
```

You could declare the same add function with the def keyword, but it would be slightly more verbose:

```
>>> def add(x, y):
...     return x + y
>>> add(5, 3)
8
```

Now you might be wondering, "Why the big fuss about lambdas? If they're just a slightly more concise version of declaring functions with def, what's the big deal?"

Take a look at the following example and keep the words *function expression* in your head while you do that:

```
>>> (lambda x, y: x + y)(5, 3)
8
```

Okay, what happened here? I just used lambda to define an "add" function inline and then immediately called it with the arguments 5 and 3.

Conceptually, the *lambda expression* `lambda x, y: x + y` is the same as declaring a function with `def`, but just written inline. The key difference here is that I didn't have to bind the function object to a name before I used it. I simply stated the expression I wanted to compute as part of a lambda, and then immediately evaluated it by calling the lambda expression like a regular function.

Before you move on, you might want to play with the previous code example a little to really let the meaning of it sink in. I still remember this taking me awhile to wrap my head around. So don't worry about spending a few minutes in an interpreter session on this. It'll be worth it.

There's another syntactic difference between lambdas and regular function definitions. Lambda functions are restricted to a single expression. This means a lambda function can't use statements or annotations—not even a `return` statement.

How do you return values from lambdas then? Executing a lambda function evaluates its expression and then automatically returns the expression's result, so there's always an *implicit* return statement. That's why some people refer to lambdas as *single expression functions*.

Lambdas You Can Use

When should you use lambda functions in your code? Technically, any time you're expected to supply a function object you can use a lambda expression. And because lambdas can be anonymous, you don't even need to assign them to a name first.

This can provide a handy and "unbureaucratic" shortcut to defining a function in Python. My most frequent use case for lambdas is writing short and concise *key funcs* for sorting iterables by an alternate key:

```
>>> tuples = [(1, 'd'), (2, 'b'), (4, 'a'), (3, 'c')]
>>> sorted(tuples, key=lambda x: x[1])
[(4, 'a'), (2, 'b'), (3, 'c'), (1, 'd')]
```

In the above example, we're sorting a list of tuples by the second value in each tuple. In this case, the lambda function provides a quick way to modify the sort order. Here's another sorting example you can play with:

```
>>> sorted(range(-5, 6), key=lambda x: x * x)
[0, -1, 1, -2, 2, -3, 3, -4, 4, -5, 5]
```

Both examples I showed you have more concise implementations in Python using the built-in operator.itemgetter() and abs() functions. But I hope you can see how using a lambda gives you much more flexibility. Want to sort a sequence by some arbitrary computed key? No problem. Now you know how to do it.

Here's another interesting thing about lambdas: Just like regular nested functions, lambdas also work as *lexical closures*.

What's a lexical closure? It's just a fancy name for a function that remembers the values from the enclosing lexical scope even when the program flow is no longer in that scope. Here's a (fairly academic) example to illustrate the idea:

```
>>> def make_adder(n):
...     return lambda x: x + n

>>> plus_3 = make_adder(3)
>>> plus_5 = make_adder(5)

>>> plus_3(4)
7
>>> plus_5(4)
9
```

In the above example, the x + n lambda can still access the value of n even though it was defined in the make_adder function (the enclosing scope).

Sometimes, using a lambda function instead of a nested function declared with the def keyword can express the programmer's intent more clearly. But to be honest, this isn't a common occurrence—at least not in the kind of code that I like to write. So let's talk a little more about that.

But Maybe You Shouldn't...

On the one hand, I'm hoping this chapter got you interested in exploring Python's lambda functions. On the other hand, I feel like it's time to put up another caveat: Lambda functions should be used sparingly and with extraordinary care.

I know I've written my fair share of code using lambdas that looked "cool" but were actually a liability for me and my coworkers. If you're tempted to use a lambda, spend a few seconds (or minutes) to think if it is really the cleanest and most maintainable way to achieve the desired result.

For example, doing something like this to save two lines of code is just silly. Sure, technically it works and it's a nice enough "trick." But it's also going to confuse the next gal or guy that has to ship a bugfix under a tight deadline:

```
# Harmful:
>>> class Car:
...     rev = lambda self: print('Wroom!')
...     crash = lambda self: print('Boom!')

>>> my_car = Car()
>>> my_car.crash()
'Boom!'
```

I have similar feelings about complicated `map()` or `filter()` constructs using lambdas. Usually it's much cleaner to go with a list comprehension or generator expression:

```
# Harmful:
>>> list(filter(lambda x: x % 2 == 0, range(16)))
[0, 2, 4, 6, 8, 10, 12, 14]

# Better:
>>> [x for x in range(16) if x % 2 == 0]
[0, 2, 4, 6, 8, 10, 12, 14]
```

If you find yourself doing anything remotely complex with lambda expressions, consider defining a standalone function with a proper name instead.

Saving a few keystrokes won't matter in the long run, but your colleagues (and your future self) will appreciate clean and readable code more than terse wizardry.

Key Takeaways

- Lambda functions are single-expression functions that are not necessarily bound to a name (anonymous).
- Lambda functions can't use regular Python statements and always include an implicit `return` statement.
- Always ask yourself: *Would using a regular (named) function or a list comprehension offer more clarity?*

3.3 The Power of Decorators

At their core, Python's decorators allow you to extend and modify the behavior of a callable (functions, methods, and classes) *without* permanently modifying the callable itself.

Any sufficiently generic functionality you can tack on to an existing class or function's behavior makes a great use case for decoration. This includes the following:

- logging
- enforcing access control and authentication
- instrumentation and timing functions
- rate-limiting
- caching, and more

Now, why should you master the use of decorators in Python? After all, what I just mentioned sounded quite abstract, and it might be difficult to see how decorators can benefit you in your day-to-day work as a Python developer. Let me try to bring some clarity to this question by giving you a somewhat real-world example:

Imagine you've got 30 functions with business logic in your report-generating program. One rainy Monday morning your boss walks up to your desk and says: *"Happy Monday! Remember those TPS reports? I need you to add input/output logging to each step in the report generator. XYZ Corp needs it for auditing purposes. Oh, and I told them we can ship this by Wednesday."*

Depending on whether or not you've got a solid grasp on Python's decorators, this request will either send your blood pressure spiking or leave you relatively calm.

Without decorators you might be spending the next three days scrambling to modify each of those 30 functions and clutter them up with manual logging calls. Fun times, right?

If you do know your decorators however, you'll calmly smile at your boss and say: *"Don't worry Jim, I'll get it done by 2pm today."*

Right after that you'll type the code for a generic `@audit_log` decorator (that's only about 10 lines long) and quickly paste it in front of each function definition. Then you'll commit your code and grab another cup of coffee...

I'm dramatizing here, but only a little. Decorators *can be* that powerful. I'd go as far as to say that understanding decorators is a milestone for any serious Python programmer. They require a solid grasp of several advanced concepts in the language, including the properties of *first-class functions*.

I believe that the payoff for understanding how decorators work in Python can be enormous.

Sure, decorators are relatively complicated to wrap your head around for the first time, but they're a highly useful feature that you'll often encounter in third-party frameworks and the Python standard library. Explaining decorators is also a *make or break* moment for any good Python tutorial. I'll do my best here to introduce you to them step by step.

Before you dive in however, now would be an excellent moment to refresh your memory on the properties of *first-class functions* in Python. There's a chapter on them in this book, and I would encourage you to take a few minutes to review it. The most important "first-class functions" takeaways for understanding decorators are:

- **Functions are objects**—they can be assigned to variables and passed to and returned from other functions

- **Functions can be defined inside other functions**—and a child function can capture the parent function's local state (lexical closures)

Alright, are you ready to do this? Let's get started.

Python Decorator Basics

Now, what are decorators really? They "decorate" or "wrap" another function and let you execute code before and after the wrapped function runs.

Decorators allow you to define reusable building blocks that can change or extend the behavior of other functions. And, they let you do that without permanently modifying the wrapped function itself. The function's behavior changes only when it's *decorated*.

What might the implementation of a simple decorator look like? In basic terms, a decorator is *a callable that takes a callable as input and returns another callable.*

The following function has that property and could be considered the simplest decorator you could possibly write:

```python
def null_decorator(func):
    return func
```

As you can see, null_decorator is a callable (it's a function), it takes another callable as its input, and it returns the same input callable without modifying it.

Let's use it to *decorate* (or *wrap*) another function:

```python
def greet():
    return 'Hello!'

greet = null_decorator(greet)

>>> greet()
'Hello!'
```

In this example, I've defined a greet function and then immediately decorated it by running it through the null_decorator function. I know this doesn't look very useful yet. I mean, we specifically designed the null decorator to be useless, right? But in a moment this example will clarify how Python's special-case decorator syntax works.

Instead of explicitly calling `null_decorator` on `greet` and then reassigning the `greet` variable, you can use Python's @ syntax for decorating a function more conveniently:

```python
@null_decorator
def greet():
    return 'Hello!'

>>> greet()
'Hello!'
```

Putting an `@null_decorator` line in front of the function definition is the same as defining the function first and then running through the decorator. Using the @ syntax is just *syntactic sugar* and a shortcut for this commonly used pattern.

Note that using the @ syntax decorates the function immediately at definition time. This makes it difficult to access the undecorated original without brittle hacks. Therefore you might choose to decorate some functions manually in order to retain the ability to call the undecorated function as well.

Decorators Can Modify Behavior

Now that you're a little more familiar with the decorator syntax, let's write another decorator that *actually does something* and modifies the behavior of the decorated function.

Here's a slightly more complex decorator which converts the result of the decorated function to uppercase letters:

```
def uppercase(func):
    def wrapper():
        original_result = func()
        modified_result = original_result.upper()
        return modified_result
    return wrapper
```

Instead of simply returning the input function like the null decorator did, this uppercase decorator defines a new function on the fly (a closure) and uses it to *wrap* the input function in order to modify its behavior at call time.

The wrapper closure has access to the undecorated input function and it is free to execute additional code before and after calling the input function. (Technically, it doesn't even need to call the input function at all.)

Note how, up until now, the decorated function has never been executed. Actually calling the input function at this point wouldn't make any sense—you'll want the decorator to be able to modify the behavior of its input function when it eventually gets called.

You might want to let that sink in for a minute or two. I know how complicated this stuff can seem, but we'll get it sorted out together, I promise.

Time to see the uppercase decorator in action. What happens if you decorate the original greet function with it?

```
@uppercase
def greet():
    return 'Hello!'

>>> greet()
'HELLO!'
```

I hope this was the result you expected. Let's take a closer look at what just happened here. Unlike null_decorator, our uppercase decorator returns a *different function object* when it decorates a function:

```
>>> greet
<function greet at 0x10e9f0950>

>>> null_decorator(greet)
<function greet at 0x10e9f0950>

>>> uppercase(greet)
<function uppercase.<locals>.wrapper at 0x76da02f28>
```

And as you saw earlier, it needs to do that in order to modify the behavior of the decorated function when it finally gets called. The uppercase decorator is a function itself. And the only way to influence the "future behavior" of an input function it decorates is to replace (or *wrap*) the input function with a closure.

That's why uppercase defines and returns another function (the closure) that can then be called at a later time, run the original input function, and modify its result.

Decorators modify the behavior of a callable through a wrapper closure so you don't have to permanently modify the original. The original callable isn't permanently modified—its behavior changes only when decorated.

This lets you tack on reusable building blocks, like logging and other instrumentation, to existing functions and classes. It makes decorators such a powerful feature in Python that it's frequently used in the standard library and in third-party packages.

A Quick Intermission

By the way, if you feel like you need a quick coffee break or a walk around the block at this point—that's totally normal. In my opinion closures and decorators are some of the most difficult concepts to understand in Python.

Please, take your time and don't worry about figuring this out immediately. Playing through the code examples in an interpreter session one by one often helps make things sink in.

I know you can do it!

Applying Multiple Decorators to a Function

Perhaps not surprisingly, you can apply more than one decorator to a function. This accumulates their effects and it's what makes decorators so helpful as reusable building blocks.

Here's an example. The following two decorators wrap the output string of the decorated function in HTML tags. By looking at how the tags are nested, you can see which order Python uses to apply multiple decorators:

```python
def strong(func):
    def wrapper():
        return '<strong>' + func() + '</strong>'
    return wrapper

def emphasis(func):
    def wrapper():
        return '<em>' + func() + '</em>'
    return wrapper
```

Now let's take these two decorators and apply them to our greet function at the same time. You can use the regular @ syntax for that and just "stack" multiple decorators on top of a single function:

```python
@strong
@emphasis
```

```
def greet():
    return 'Hello!'
```

What output do you expect to see if you run the decorated function? Will the @emphasis decorator add its <em> tag first, or does @strong have precedence? Here's what happens when you call the decorated function:

```
>>> greet()
'<strong><em>Hello!</em></strong>'
```

This clearly shows in what order the decorators were applied: from *bottom to top*. First, the input function was wrapped by the @emphasis decorator, and then the resulting (decorated) function got wrapped again by the @strong decorator.

To help me remember this bottom to top order, I like to call this behavior *decorator stacking*. You start building the stack at the bottom and then keep adding new blocks on top to work your way upwards.

If you break down the above example and avoid the @ syntax to apply the decorators, the chain of decorator function calls looks like this:

```
decorated_greet = strong(emphasis(greet))
```

Again, you can see that the emphasis decorator is applied first and then the resulting wrapped function is wrapped again by the strong decorator.

This also means that deep levels of decorator stacking will eventually have an effect on performance because they keep adding nested function calls. In practice, this usually won't be a problem, but it's something to keep in mind if you're working on performance-intensive code that frequently uses decoration.

Decorating Functions That Accept Arguments

All examples so far only decorated a simple *nullary* greet function that didn't take any arguments whatsoever. Up until now, the decorators you saw here didn't have to deal with forwarding arguments to the input function.

If you try to apply one of these decorators to a function that takes arguments, it will not work correctly. How do you decorate a function that takes arbitrary arguments?

This is where Python's *args and **kwargs feature[3] for dealing with variable numbers of arguments comes in handy. The following proxy decorator takes advantage of that:

```python
def proxy(func):
    def wrapper(*args, **kwargs):
        return func(*args, **kwargs)
    return wrapper
```

There are two notable things going on with this decorator:

- It uses the * and ** operators in the wrapper closure definition to collect all positional and keyword arguments and stores them in variables (args and kwargs).

- The wrapper closure then forwards the collected arguments to the original input function using the * and ** "argument unpacking" operators.

It's a bit unfortunate that the meaning of the star and double-star operators is overloaded and changes depending on the context they're used in, but I hope you get the idea.

---

[3]cf. "Fun With *args and **kwargs" chapter

Let's expand the technique laid out by the proxy decorator into a more useful practical example. Here's a trace decorator that logs function arguments and results during execution time:

```python
def trace(func):
    def wrapper(*args, **kwargs):
        print(f'TRACE: calling {func.__name__}() '
              f'with {args}, {kwargs}')

        original_result = func(*args, **kwargs)

        print(f'TRACE: {func.__name__}() '
              f'returned {original_result!r}')

        return original_result
    return wrapper
```

Decorating a function with trace and then calling it will print the arguments passed to the decorated function and its return value. This is still somewhat of a "toy" example—but in a pinch it makes a great debugging aid:

```python
@trace
def say(name, line):
    return f'{name}: {line}'

>>> say('Jane', 'Hello, World')
'TRACE: calling say() with ("Jane", "Hello, World"), {}'
'TRACE: say() returned "Jane: Hello, World"'
'Jane: Hello, World'
```

Speaking of debugging, there are some things you should keep in mind when debugging decorators:

How to Write "Debuggable" Decorators

When you use a decorator, really what you're doing is replacing one function with another. One downside of this process is that it "hides" some of the metadata attached to the original (undecorated) function.

For example, the original function name, its docstring, and parameter list are hidden by the wrapper closure:

```
def greet():
    """Return a friendly greeting."""
    return 'Hello!'

decorated_greet = uppercase(greet)
```

If you try to access any of that function metadata, you'll see the wrapper closure's metadata instead:

```
>>> greet.__name__
'greet'
>>> greet.__doc__
'Return a friendly greeting.'

>>> decorated_greet.__name__
'wrapper'
>>> decorated_greet.__doc__
None
```

This makes debugging and working with the Python interpreter awkward and challenging. Thankfully there's a quick fix for this: the functools.wraps decorator included in Python's standard library.[4]

You can use functools.wraps in your own decorators to copy over the lost metadata from the undecorated function to the decorator closure. Here's an example:

---

[4]cf. Python Docs: "functools.wraps"

```
import functools

def uppercase(func):
    @functools.wraps(func)
    def wrapper():
        return func().upper()
    return wrapper
```

Applying `functools.wraps` to the wrapper closure returned by the decorator carries over the docstring and other metadata of the input function:

```
@uppercase
def greet():
    """Return a friendly greeting."""
    return 'Hello!'

>>> greet.__name__
'greet'
>>> greet.__doc__
'Return a friendly greeting.'
```

As a best practice, I'd recommend that you use `functools.wraps` in all of the decorators you write yourself. It doesn't take much time and it will save you (and others) debugging headaches down the road.

Oh, and congratulations—you've made it all the way to the end of this complicated chapter and learned a whole lot about decorators in Python. Great job!

Key Takeaways

- Decorators define reusable building blocks you can apply to a callable to modify its behavior without permanently modifying the callable itself.

- The @ syntax is just a shorthand for calling the decorator on an input function. Multiple decorators on a single function are applied bottom to top (*decorator stacking*).
- As a debugging best practice, use the `functools.wraps` helper in your own decorators to carry over metadata from the undecorated callable to the decorated one.
- Just like any other tool in the software development toolbox, decorators are not a cure-all and they should not be overused. It's important to balance the need to "get stuff done" with the goal of "not getting tangled up in a horrible, unmaintainable mess of a code base."

3.4 Fun With *args and **kwargs

I once pair-programmed with a smart Pythonista who would exclaim "argh!" and "kwargh!" every time he typed out a function definition with optional or keyword parameters. We got along great otherwise. I guess that's what programming in academia does to people eventually.

Now, while easily mocked, *args and **kwargs parameters are nevertheless a highly useful feature in Python. And understanding their potency will make you a more effective developer.

So what are *args and **kwargs parameters used for? They allow a function to accept *optional* arguments, so you can create flexible APIs in your modules and classes:

```python
def foo(required, *args, **kwargs):
    print(required)
    if args:
        print(args)
    if kwargs:
        print(kwargs)
```

The above function requires at least one argument called "required," but it can accept extra positional and keyword arguments as well.

If we call the function with additional arguments, args will collect extra positional arguments as a tuple because the parameter name has a * prefix.

Likewise, kwargs will collect extra keyword arguments as a dictionary because the parameter name has a ** prefix.

Both args and kwargs can be empty if no extra arguments are passed to the function.

As we call the function with various combinations of arguments, you'll see how Python collects them inside the args and kwargs parameters according to whether they're positional or keyword arguments:

```
>>> foo()
TypeError:
"foo() missing 1 required positional arg: 'required'"

>>> foo('hello')
hello

>>> foo('hello', 1, 2, 3)
hello
(1, 2, 3)

>>> foo('hello', 1, 2, 3, key1='value', key2=999)
hello
(1, 2, 3)
{'key1': 'value', 'key2': 999}
```

I want to make it clear that calling the parameters args and kwargs is simply a naming convention. The previous example would work just as well if you called them *parms and **argv. The actual syntax is just the asterisk (*) or double asterisk (**), respectively.

However, I recommend that you stick with the accepted naming convention to avoid confusion. (And to get a chance to yell "argh!" and "kwargh!" every once in a while.)

Forwarding Optional or Keyword Arguments

It's possible to pass optional or keyword parameters from one function to another. You can do so by using the argument-unpacking operators * and ** when calling the function you want to forward arguments to.[5]

---

[5]cf. "Function Argument Unpacking" chapter

This also gives you an opportunity to modify the arguments before you pass them along. Here's an example:

```python
def foo(x, *args, **kwargs):
    kwargs['name'] = 'Alice'
    new_args = args + ('extra', )
    bar(x, *new_args, **kwargs)
```

This technique can be useful for subclassing and writing wrapper functions. For example, you can use it to extend the behavior of a parent class without having to replicate the full signature of its constructor in the child class. This can be quite convenient if you're working with an API that might change outside of your control:

```python
class Car:
    def __init__(self, color, mileage):
        self.color = color
        self.mileage = mileage

class AlwaysBlueCar(Car):
    def __init__(self, *args, **kwargs):
        super().__init__(*args, **kwargs)
        self.color = 'blue'

>>> AlwaysBlueCar('green', 48392).color
'blue'
```

The AlwaysBlueCar constructor simply passes on all arguments to its parent class and then overrides an internal attribute. This means if the parent class constructor changes, there's a good chance that AlwaysBlueCar would still function as intended.

The downside here is that the AlwaysBlueCar constructor now has a rather unhelpful signature—we don't know what arguments it expects without looking up the parent class.

Typically you wouldn't use this technique with your own class hierarchies. The more likely scenario would be that you'll want to modify or override behavior in some external class which you don't control.

But this is always dangerous territory, so best be careful (or you might soon have yet another reason to scream "argh!").

One more scenario where this technique is potentially helpful is writing wrapper functions such as decorators. There you typically also want to accept arbitrary arguments to be passed through to the wrapped function.

And, if we can do it without having to copy and paste the original function's signature, that might be more maintainable:

```python
def trace(f):
    @functools.wraps(f)
    def decorated_function(*args, **kwargs):
        print(f, args, kwargs)
        result = f(*args, **kwargs)
        print(result)
    return decorated_function

@trace
def greet(greeting, name):
    return '{}, {}!'.format(greeting, name)

>>> greet('Hello', 'Bob')
<function greet at 0x1031c9158> ('Hello', 'Bob') {}
'Hello, Bob!'
```

With techniques like this one, it's sometimes difficult to balance the idea of making your code explicit enough and yet adhere to the *Don't Repeat Yourself (DRY)* principle. This will always be a tough choice to make. If you can get a second opinion from a colleague, I'd encourage you to ask for one.

Key Takeaways

- *args and **kwargs let you write functions with a variable number of arguments in Python.
- *args collects extra positional arguments as a tuple. **kwargs collects the extra keyword arguments as a dictionary.
- The actual syntax is * and **. Calling them args and kwargs is just a convention (and one you should stick to).

3.5 Function Argument Unpacking

A really cool but slightly arcane feature is the ability to "unpack" function arguments from sequences and dictionaries with the * and ** operators.

Let's define a simple function to work with as an example:

```python
def print_vector(x, y, z):
    print('<%s, %s, %s>' % (x, y, z))
```

As you can see, this function takes three arguments (x, y, and z) and prints them in a nicely formatted way. We might use this function to pretty-print 3-dimensional vectors in our program:

```python
>>> print_vector(0, 1, 0)
<0, 1, 0>
```

Now depending on which data structure we choose to represent 3D vectors with, printing them with our `print_vector` function might feel a little awkward. For example, if our vectors are represented as tuples or lists we must explicitly specify the index for each component when printing them:

```python
>>> tuple_vec = (1, 0, 1)
>>> list_vec = [1, 0, 1]
>>> print_vector(tuple_vec[0],
                 tuple_vec[1],
                 tuple_vec[2])
<1, 0, 1>
```

Using a normal function call with separate arguments seems unnecessarily verbose and cumbersome. Wouldn't it be much nicer if we could just "explode" a vector object into its three components and pass everything to the `print_vector` function all at once?

(Of course, you could simply redefine print_vector so that it takes a single parameter representing a vector object—but for the sake of having a simple example, we'll ignore that option for now.)

Thankfully, there's a better way to handle this situation in Python with *Function Argument Unpacking* using the * operator:

```
>>> print_vector(*tuple_vec)
<1, 0, 1>
>>> print_vector(*list_vec)
<1, 0, 1>
```

Putting a * before an iterable in a function call will *unpack* it and pass its elements as separate positional arguments to the called function.

This technique works for any iterable, including generator expressions. Using the * operator on a generator consumes all elements from the generator and passes them to the function:

```
>>> genexpr = (x * x for x in range(3))
>>> print_vector(*genexpr)
```

Besides the * operator for unpacking sequences like tuples, lists, and generators into positional arguments, there's also the ** operator for unpacking keyword arguments from dictionaries. Imagine our vector was represented as the following dict object:

```
>>> dict_vec = {'y': 0, 'z': 1, 'x': 1}
```

We could pass this dict to print_vector in much the same way using the ** operator for unpacking:

```
>>> print_vector(**dict_vec)
<1, 0, 1>
```

Because dictionaries are unordered, this matches up dictionary values and function arguments based on the dictionary keys: the x argument receives the value associated with the 'x' key in the dictionary.

If you were to use the single asterisk (*) operator to unpack the dictionary, keys would be passed to the function in random order instead:

```
>>> print_vector(*dict_vec)
<y, x, z>
```

Python's function argument unpacking feature gives you a lot of flexibility for free. Often this means you won't have to implement a class for a data type needed by your program. As a result, using simple built-in data structures like tuples or lists will suffice and help reduce the complexity of your code.

Key Takeaways

- The * and ** operators can be used to "unpack" function arguments from sequences and dictionaries.
- Using argument unpacking effectively can help you write more flexible interfaces for your modules and functions.

3.6 Nothing to Return Here

Python adds an implicit `return None` statement to the end of any function. Therefore, if a function doesn't specify a return value, it returns None by default.

This means you can replace `return None` statements with bare return statements or even leave them out completely and still get the same result:

```python
def foo1(value):
    if value:
        return value
    else:
        return None

def foo2(value):
    """Bare return statement implies `return None`"""
    if value:
        return value
    else:
        return

def foo3(value):
    """Missing return statement implies `return None`"""
    if value:
        return value
```

All three functions properly return None if you pass them a falsy value as the sole argument:

```python
>>> type(foo1(0))
<class 'NoneType'>

>>> type(foo2(0))
<class 'NoneType'>
```

```
>>> type(foo3(0))
<class 'NoneType'>
```

Now, when is it a good idea to use this feature in your own Python code?

My rule of thumb is that if a function *doesn't have a return value* (other languages would call this a *procedure*), then I will leave out the `return` statement. Adding one would just be superfluous and confusing. An example for a procedure would be Python's built-in `print` function which is only called for its side-effects (printing text) and never for its return value.

Let's take a function like Python's built-in `sum`. It clearly has a logical return value, and typically `sum` wouldn't get called only for its side-effects. Its purpose is to add a sequence of numbers together and then deliver the result. Now, if a function *does* have a return value from a logical point of view, then you need to decide whether to use an implicit return or not.

On the one hand, you could argue that omitting an explicit `return` None statement makes the code more concise and therefore easier to read and understand. Subjectively, you might also say it makes the code "prettier."

On the other hand, it might surprise some programmers that Python behaves this way. When it comes to writing clean and maintainable code, surprising behavior is rarely a good sign.

For example, I've been using an "implicit return statement" in one of the code samples in an earlier revision of the book. I didn't mention what I was doing—I just wanted a nice short code sample to explain some other feature in Python.

Eventually I started getting a steady stream of emails pointing me to "the missing return statement" in that code example. Python's implicit return behavior was clearly *not* obvious to everybody and was a distraction in this case. I added a note to make it clear what was going on, and the emails stopped.

Don't get me wrong—I love writing clean and "beautiful" code as much as anyone. And I also used to feel strongly that programmers should know the ins and outs of the language they're working with.

But when you consider the maintenance impact of even such a simple misunderstanding, it might make sense to lean towards writing more explicit and clear code. After all, *code is communication.*

Key Takeaways

- If a function doesn't specify a return value, it returns None. Whether to explicitly return None is a stylistic decision.
- This is a core Python feature but your code might communicate its intent more clearly with an explicit `return` None statement.

Chapter 4

Classes & OOP

4.1 Object Comparisons: "is" vs "=="

When I was a kid, our neighbors had two twin cats. They looked seemingly identical—the same charcoal fur and the same piercing green eyes. Some personality quirks aside, you couldn't tell them apart just from looking at them. But of course, they were two different cats, two separate beings, even though they looked exactly the same.

That brings me to the difference in meaning between *equal* and *identical*. And this difference is crucial to understanding how Python's is and == comparison operators behave.

The == operator compares by checking for *equality*: if these cats were Python objects and we compared them with the == operator, we'd get "both cats are equal" as an answer.

The is operator, however, compares *identities*: if we compared our cats with the is operator, we'd get "these are two different cats" as an answer.

But before I get all tangled up in this ball-of-twine cat analogy, let's take a look at some real Python code.

First, we'll create a new list object and name it a, and then define another variable (b) that points to the same list object:

```
>>> a = [1, 2, 3]
>>> b = a
```

Let's inspect these two variables. We can see that they point to identical-looking lists:

```
>>> a
[1, 2, 3]
>>> b
[1, 2, 3]
```

Because the two list objects look the same, we'll get the expected result when we compare them for equality by using the == operator:

```
>>> a == b
True
```

However, that doesn't tell us whether a and b are actually pointing to the same object. Of course, we know they are because we assigned them earlier, but suppose we didn't know—how might we find out?

The answer is to compare both variables with the is operator. This confirms that both variables are in fact pointing to one list object:

```
>>> a is b
True
```

Let's see what happens when we create an identical copy of our list object. We can do that by calling list() on the existing list to create a copy we'll name c:

```
>>> c = list(a)
```

Again you'll see that the new list we just created looks identical to the list object pointed to by a and b:

```
>>> c
[1, 2, 3]
```

Now this is where it gets interesting. Let's compare our list copy c with the initial list a using the == operator. What answer do you expect to see?

```
>>> a == c
True
```

Okay, I hope this was what you expected. What this result tells us is that c and a have the same contents. They're considered equal by Python. But are they actually pointing to the same object? Let's find out with the is operator:

```
>>> a is c
False
```

Boom! This is where we get a different result. Python is telling us that c and a are pointing to two different objects, even though their contents might be the same.

So, to recap, let's try and break down the difference between is and == into two short definitions:

- An is expression evaluates to True if two variables point to the same (identical) object.

- An == expression evaluates to True if the objects referred to by the variables are equal (have the same contents).

Just remember to think of twin cats (dogs should work, too) whenever you need to decide between using is and == in Python. If you do that, you'll be fine.

4.2 String Conversion (Every Class Needs a __repr__)

When you define a custom class in Python and then try to print one of its instances to the console (or inspect it in an interpreter session), you get a relatively unsatisfying result. The default "to string" conversion behavior is basic and lacks detail:

```python
class Car:
    def __init__(self, color, mileage):
        self.color = color
        self.mileage = mileage

>>> my_car = Car('red', 37281)
>>> print(my_car)
<__console__.Car object at 0x109b73da0>
>>> my_car
<__console__.Car object at 0x109b73da0>
```

By default all you get is a string containing the class name and the id of the object instance (which is the object's memory address in CPython.) That's better than *nothing*, but it's also not very useful.

You might find yourself trying to work around this by printing attributes of the class directly, or even by adding a custom to_string() method to your classes:

```python
>>> print(my_car.color, my_car.mileage)
red 37281
```

The general idea here is the right one—but it ignores the conventions and built-in mechanisms Python uses to handle how objects are represented as strings.

Instead of building your own to-string conversion machinery, you'll be better off adding the __str__ and __repr__ "dunder" methods to your class. They are the Pythonic way to control how objects are converted to strings in different situations.[1]

Let's take a look at how these methods work in practice. To get started, we're going to add a __str__ method to the Car class we defined earlier:

```python
class Car:
    def __init__(self, color, mileage):
        self.color = color
        self.mileage = mileage

    def __str__(self):
        return f'a {self.color} car'
```

When you try printing or inspecting a Car instance now, you'll get a different, slightly improved result:

```python
>>> my_car = Car('red', 37281)
>>> print(my_car)
'a red car'
>>> my_car
<__console__.Car object at 0x109ca24e0>
```

Inspecting the car object in the console still gives us the previous result containing the object's id. But *printing* the object resulted in the string returned by the __str__ method we added.

__str__ is one of Python's "dunder" (double-underscore) methods and gets called when you try to convert an object into a string through the various means that are available:

```python
>>> print(my_car)
a red car
```

---

[1] cf. Python Docs: "The Python Data Model"

```
>>> str(my_car)
'a red car'
>>> '{}'.format(my_car)
'a red car'
```

With a proper __str__ implementation, you won't have to worry about printing object attributes directly or writing a separate to_string() function. It's the Pythonic way to control string conversion.

By the way, some people refer to Python's "dunder" methods as "magic methods." But these methods are not supposed to be *magical* in any way. The fact that these methods start and end in double underscores is simply a naming convention to flag them as core Python features. It also helps avoid naming collisions with your own methods and attributes. The object constructor __init__ follows the same convention, and there's nothing magical or arcane about it.

Don't be afraid to use Python's dunder methods—they're meant to help you.

__str__ vs __repr__

Now, our string conversion story doesn't end there. Did you see how inspecting my_car in an interpreter session still gave that odd <Car object at 0x109ca24e0> result?

This happened because there are actually *two* dunder methods that control how objects are converted to strings in Python 3. The first one is __str__, and you just learned about it. The second one is __repr__, and the way it works is similar to __str__, but it is used in different situations. (Python 2.x also has a __unicode__ method that I'll touch on a little later.)

Here's a simple experiment you can use to get a feel for when __str__ or __repr__ is used. Let's redefine our car class so it contains both *to-string* dunder methods with outputs that are easy to distinguish:

```
class Car:
    def __init__(self, color, mileage):
        self.color = color
        self.mileage = mileage

    def __repr__(self):
        return '__repr__ for Car'

    def __str__(self):
        return '__str__ for Car'
```

Now, when you play through the previous examples you can see which method controls the string conversion result in each case:

```
>>> my_car = Car('red', 37281)
>>> print(my_car)
__str__ for Car
>>> '{}'.format(my_car)
'__str__ for Car'
>>> my_car
__repr__ for Car
```

This experiment confirms that inspecting an object in a Python interpreter session simply prints the result of the object's __repr__.

Interestingly, containers like lists and dicts always use the result of __repr__ to represent the objects they contain. Even if you call str on the container itself:

```
str([my_car])
'[__repr__ for Car]'
```

To manually choose between both string conversion methods, for example, to express your code's intent more clearly, it's best to use the built-in str() and repr() functions. Using them is preferable over calling the object's __str__ or __repr__ directly, as it looks nicer and gives the same result:

```
>>> str(my_car)
'__str__ for Car'
>>> repr(my_car)
'__repr__ for Car'
```

Even with this investigation complete, you might be wondering what the "real-world" difference is between __str__ and __repr__. They both seem to serve the same purpose, so it might be unclear when to use each.

With questions like that, it's usually a good idea to look into what the Python standard library does. Time to devise another experiment. We'll create a datetime.date object and find out how it uses __repr__ and __str__ to control string conversion:

```
>>> import datetime
>>> today = datetime.date.today()
```

The result of the date object's __str__ function should primarily be *readable*. It's meant to return a concise textual representation for human consumption—something you'd feel comfortable displaying to a user. Therefore, we get something that looks like an ISO date format when we call str() on the date object:

```
>>> str(today)
'2017-02-02'
```

With __repr__, the idea is that its result should be, above all, *unambiguous*. The resulting string is intended more as a debugging aid for developers. And for that it needs to be as explicit as possible about what this object is. That's why you'll get a more elaborate result calling repr() on the object. It even includes the full module and class name:

```
>>> repr(today)
'datetime.date(2017, 2, 2)'
```

We could copy and paste the string returned by __repr__ and execute it as valid Python to recreate the original date object. This is a neat approach and a good goal to keep in mind while writing your own reprs.

On the other hand, I find that it is quite difficult to put into practice. Usually it won't be worth the trouble and it'll just create extra work for you. My rule of thumb is to make my __repr__ strings unambiguous and helpful for developers, but I don't expect them to be able to restore an object's complete state.

Why Every Class Needs a __repr__

If you don't add a __str__ method, Python falls back on the result of __repr__ when looking for __str__. Therefore, I recommend that you always add at least a __repr__ method to your classes. This will guarantee a useful string conversion result in almost all cases, with a minimum of implementation work.

Here's how to add basic string conversion support to your classes quickly and efficiently. For our Car class we might start with the following __repr__:

```
def __repr__(self):
    return f'Car({self.color!r}, {self.mileage!r})'
```

Please note that I'm using the !r conversion flag to make sure the output string uses repr(self.color) and repr(self.mileage) instead of str(self.color) and str(self.mileage).

This works nicely, but one downside is that we've repeated the class name inside the format string. A trick you can use here to avoid this repetition is to use the object's __class__.__name__ attribute, which will always reflect the class' name as a string.

The benefit is you won't have to modify the __repr__ implementation when the class name changes. This makes it easy to adhere to the *Don't Repeat Yourself (DRY)* principle:

```python
def __repr__(self):
    return (f'{self.__class__.__name__}('
            f'{self.color!r}, {self.mileage!r})')
```

The downside of this implementation is that the format string is quite long and unwieldy. But with careful formatting, you can keep the code nice and PEP 8 compliant.

With the above __repr__ implementation, we get a useful result when we inspect the object or call repr() on it directly:

```python
>>> repr(my_car)
'Car(red, 37281)'
```

Printing the object or calling str() on it returns the same string because the default __str__ implementation simply calls __repr__:

```python
>>> print(my_car)
'Car(red, 37281)'
>>> str(my_car)
'Car(red, 37281)'
```

I believe this approach provides the most value with a modest amount of implementation work. It's also a fairly cookie-cutter approach that can be applied without much deliberation. For this reason, I always try to add a basic __repr__ implementation to my classes.

Here's a complete example for Python 3, including an optional __str__ implementation:

```python
class Car:
    def __init__(self, color, mileage):
        self.color = color
        self.mileage = mileage

    def __repr__(self):
        return (f'{self.__class__.__name__}('
                f'{self.color!r}, {self.mileage!r})')

    def __str__(self):
        return f'a {self.color} car'
```

Python 2.x Differences: __unicode__

In Python 3 there's one data type to represent text across the board: str. It holds unicode characters and can represent most of the world's writing systems.

Python 2.x uses a different data model for strings.[2] There are two types to represent text: str, which is limited to the ASCII character set, and unicode, which is equivalent to Python 3's str.

Due to this difference, there's yet another dunder method in the mix for controlling string conversion in Python 2: __unicode__. In Python 2, __str__ returns *bytes*, whereas __unicode__ returns *characters*.

For most intents and purposes, __unicode__ is the newer and preferred method to control string conversion. There's also a built-in unicode() function to go along with it. It calls the respective dunder method, similar to how str() and repr() work.

So far so good. Now, it gets a little more quirky when you look at the rules for when __str__ and __unicode__ are called in Python 2:

The print statement and str() call __str__. The unicode() built-

---

[2]cf. Python 2 Docs: "Data Model"

in calls __unicode__ if it exists, and otherwise falls back to __str__ and decodes the result with the system text encoding.

Compared to Python 3, these special cases complicate the text conversion rules somewhat. But there is a way to simplify things again for practical purposes. Unicode is the preferred and future-proof way of handling text in your Python programs.

So generally, what I would recommend you do in Python 2.x is to put all of your string formatting code inside the __unicode__ method and then create a stub __str__ implementation that returns the unicode representation encoded as UTF-8:

```python
def __str__(self):
    return unicode(self).encode('utf-8')
```

The __str__ stub will be the same for most classes you write, so you can just copy and paste it around as needed (or put it into a base class where it makes sense). All of your string conversion code that is meant for non-developer use then lives in __unicode__.

Here's a complete example for Python 2.x:

```python
class Car(object):
    def __init__(self, color, mileage):
        self.color = color
        self.mileage = mileage

    def __repr__(self):
        return '{}({!r}, {!r})'.format(
            self.__class__.__name__,
            self.color, self.mileage)

    def __unicode__(self):
        return u'a {self.color} car'.format(
            self=self)
```

```
def __str__(self):
    return unicode(self).encode('utf-8')
```

Key Takeaways

- You can control to-string conversion in your own classes using the __str__ and __repr__ "dunder" methods.
- The result of __str__ should be readable. The result of __repr__ should be unambiguous.
- Always add a __repr__ to your classes. The default implementation for __str__ just calls __repr__.
- Use __unicode__ instead of __str__ in Python 2.

4.3 Defining Your Own Exception Classes

When I started using Python, I was hesitant to write custom exception classes in my code. But defining your own error types can be of great value. You'll make potential error cases stand out clearly, and as a result, your functions and modules will become more maintainable. You can also use custom error types to provide additional debugging information.

All of this will improve your Python code and make it easier to understand, easier to debug, and more maintainable. Defining your own exception classes is not that hard when you break it down to a few simple examples. In this chapter I'll walk you through the main points you need to remember.

Let's say you wanted to validate an input string representing a person's name in your application. A toy example for a name validator function might look like this:

```python
def validate(name):
    if len(name) < 10:
        raise ValueError
```

If the validation fails, it throws a `ValueError` exception. That seems fitting and kind of Pythonic already. So far, so good.

However, there's a downside to using a "high-level" generic exception class like `ValueError`. Imagine one of your teammates calls this function as part of a library and doesn't know much about its internals. When a name fails to validate, it'll look like this in the debug stack trace:

```python
>>> validate('joe')
Traceback (most recent call last):
  File "<input>", line 1, in <module>
```

```
    validate('joe')
  File "<input>", line 3, in validate
    raise ValueError
ValueError
```

This stack trace isn't really all that helpful. Sure, we know that some-thing went wrong and that the problem had to do with an "incorrect value" of sorts, but to be able to fix the problem your teammate almost certainly has to look up the implementation of validate(). However, reading code costs time. And it can add up quickly.

Luckily we can do better. Let's introduce a custom exception type to represent a failed name validation. We'll base our new exception class on Python's built-in ValueError, but make it speak for itself by giving it a more explicit name:

```
class NameTooShortError(ValueError):
    pass

def validate(name):
    if len(name) < 10:
        raise NameTooShortError(name)
```

Now we have a "self-documenting" NameTooShortError excep-tion type that extends the built-in ValueError class. Generally, you'll want to either derive your custom exceptions from the root Exception class or the other built-in Python exceptions like ValueError or TypeError—whicever feels appropriate.

Also, see how we're now passing the name variable to the constructor of our custom exception class when we instantiate it inside validate? The new implementation results in a much nicer stack trace for your colleague:

```
>>> validate('jane')
Traceback (most recent call last):
  File "<input>", line 1, in <module>
    validate('jane')
  File "<input>", line 3, in validate
    raise NameTooShortError(name)
NameTooShortError: jane
```

Once again, try to put yourself in your teammate's shoes. Custom exception classes make it much easier to understand what's going on when things go wrong (and eventually they always do).

The same is true even if you're working on a code base all by yourself. A few weeks or months down the road you'll have a much easier time maintaining your code if it's well-structured.

By spending just 30 seconds on defining a simple exception class, this code snippet became much more communicative already. But let's keep going. There's more to cover.

Whenever you're publicly releasing a Python package, or even if you're creating a reusable module for your company, it's good practice to create a custom exception base class for the module and then derive all of your other exceptions from it.

Here's how to create a custom exception hierarchy for all exceptions in a module or package. The first step is to declare a base class that all of our concrete errors will inherit from:

```
class BaseValidationError(ValueError):
    pass
```

Now, all of our "real" error classes can be derived from the base error class. This gives a nice and clean exception hierarchy with little extra effort:

```python
class NameTooShortError(BaseValidationError):
    pass

class NameTooLongError(BaseValidationError):
    pass

class NameTooCuteError(BaseValidationError):
    pass
```

For example, this allows users of your package to write *try...except* statements that can handle all of the errors from this package without having to catch them manually:

```python
try:
    validate(name)
except BaseValidationError as err:
    handle_validation_error(err)
```

People can still catch more specific exceptions that way, but if they don't want to, at least they won't have to resort to snapping up all exceptions with a catchall except statement. This is generally considered an anti-pattern—it can silently swallow and hide unrelated errors and make your programs much harder to debug.

Of course you can take this idea further and logically group your exceptions into fine grained sub-hierarchies. But be careful—it's easy to introduce unnecessary complexity by going overboard with this.

In conclusion, defining custom exception classes makes it easier for your users to adopt an *it's easier to ask for forgiveness than permission* (EAFP) coding style that's considered more Pythonic.

Key Takeaways

- Defining your own exception types will state your code's intent more clearly and make it easier to debug.

- Derive your custom exceptions from Python's built-in Exception class or from more specific exception classes like ValueError or KeyError.
- You can use inheritance to define logically grouped exception hierarchies.

4.4 Cloning Objects for Fun and Profit

Assignment statements in Python do not create copies of objects, they only bind names to an object. For immutable objects, that usually doesn't make a difference.

But for working with mutable objects or collections of mutable objects, you might be looking for a way to create "real copies" or "clones" of these objects.

Essentially, you'll sometimes want copies that you can modify *without* automatically modifying the original at the same time. In this chapter I'm going to give you the rundown on how to copy or "clone" objects in Python and some of the caveats involved.

Let's start by looking at how to copy Python's built-in collections. Python's built-in mutable collections like lists, dicts, and sets can be copied by calling their factory functions on an existing collection:

```
new_list = list(original_list)
new_dict = dict(original_dict)
new_set = set(original_set)
```

However, this method won't work for custom objects and, on top of that, it only creates *shallow copies*. For compound objects like lists, dicts, and sets, there's an important difference between *shallow* and *deep* copying:

A *shallow copy* means constructing a new collection object and then populating it with references to the child objects found in the original. In essence, a shallow copy is only *one level deep*. The copying process does not recurse and therefore won't create copies of the child objects themselves.

A *deep copy* makes the copying process recursive. It means first constructing a new collection object and then recursively populating it with copies of the child objects found in the original. Copying an object this way walks the whole object tree to create a fully independent clone of the original object and all of its children.

I know, that was a bit of a mouthful. So let's look at some examples to drive home this difference between deep and shallow copies.

Making Shallow Copies

In the example below, we'll create a new nested list and then *shallowly* copy it with the list() factory function:

```
>>> xs = [[1, 2, 3], [4, 5, 6], [7, 8, 9]]
>>> ys = list(xs)  # Make a shallow copy
```

This means ys will now be a new and independent object with the same contents as xs. You can verify this by inspecting both objects:

```
>>> xs
[[1, 2, 3], [4, 5, 6], [7, 8, 9]]
>>> ys
[[1, 2, 3], [4, 5, 6], [7, 8, 9]]
```

To confirm ys really is independent from the original, let's devise a little experiment. You could try and add a new sublist to the original (xs) and then check to make sure this modification didn't affect the copy (ys):

```
>>> xs.append(['new sublist'])
>>> xs
[[1, 2, 3], [4, 5, 6], [7, 8, 9], ['new sublist']]
>>> ys
[[1, 2, 3], [4, 5, 6], [7, 8, 9]]
```

As you can see, this had the expected effect. Modifying the copied list at a "superficial" level was no problem at all.

However, because we only created a *shallow* copy of the original list, ys still contains references to the original child objects stored in xs.

These children were *not* copied. They were merely referenced again in the copied list.

Therefore, when you modify one of the child objects in xs, this modification will be reflected in ys as well—that's because *both lists share the same child objects*. The copy is only a shallow, one level deep copy:

```
>>> xs[1][0] = 'X'
>>> xs
[[1, 2, 3], ['X', 5, 6], [7, 8, 9], ['new sublist']]
>>> ys
[[1, 2, 3], ['X', 5, 6], [7, 8, 9]]
```

In the above example we (seemingly) only made a change to xs. But it turns out that *both* sublists at index 1 in xs *and* ys were modified. Again, this happened because we had only created a *shallow* copy of the original list.

Had we created a *deep* copy of xs in the first step, both objects would've been fully independent. This is the practical difference between shallow and deep copies of objects.

Now you know how to create shallow copies of some of the built-in collection classes, and you know the difference between shallow and deep copying. The questions we still want answers for are:

- How can you create deep copies of built-in collections?
- How can you create copies (shallow and deep) of arbitrary objects, including custom classes?

The answer to these questions lies in the copy module in the Python standard library. This module provides a simple interface for creating shallow and deep copies of arbitrary Python objects.

Making Deep Copies

Let's repeat the previous list-copying example, but with one important difference. This time we're going to create a *deep* copy using the deepcopy() function defined in the copy module instead:

```
>>> import copy
>>> xs = [[1, 2, 3], [4, 5, 6], [7, 8, 9]]
>>> zs = copy.deepcopy(xs)
```

When you inspect xs and its clone zs that we created with copy.deepcopy(), you'll see that they both look identical again—just like in the previous example:

```
>>> xs
[[1, 2, 3], [4, 5, 6], [7, 8, 9]]
>>> zs
[[1, 2, 3], [4, 5, 6], [7, 8, 9]]
```

However, if you make a modification to one of the child objects in the original object (xs), you'll see that this modification won't affect the deep copy (zs).

Both objects, the original and the copy, are fully independent this time. xs was cloned recursively, including all of its child objects:

```
>>> xs[1][0] = 'X'
>>> xs
[[1, 2, 3], ['X', 5, 6], [7, 8, 9]]
>>> zs
[[1, 2, 3], [4, 5, 6], [7, 8, 9]]
```

You might want to take some time to sit down with the Python interpreter and play through these examples right about now. Wrapping your head around copying objects is easier when you get to experience and play with the examples firsthand.

By the way, you can also create shallow copies using a function in the copy module. The copy.copy() function creates shallow copies of objects.

This is useful if you need to clearly communicate that you're creating a shallow copy somewhere in your code. Using copy.copy() lets you indicate this fact. However, for built-in collections it's considered more Pythonic to simply use the list, dict, and set factory functions to create shallow copies.

Copying Arbitrary Objects

The question we still need to answer is how do we create copies (shallow and deep) of arbitrary objects, including custom classes. Let's take a look at that now.

Again the copy module comes to our rescue. Its copy.copy() and copy.deepcopy() functions can be used to duplicate any object.

Once again, the best way to understand how to use these is with a simple experiment. I'm going to base this on the previous list-copying example. Let's start by defining a simple 2D point class:

```python
class Point:
    def __init__(self, x, y):
        self.x = x
        self.y = y

    def __repr__(self):
        return f'Point({self.x!r}, {self.y!r})'
```

I hope you agree that this was pretty straightforward. I added a __repr__() implementation so that we can easily inspect objects created from this class in the Python interpreter.

Next up, we'll create a Point instance and then (shallowly) copy it, using the copy module:

```
>>> a = Point(23, 42)
>>> b = copy.copy(a)
```

If we inspect the contents of the original Point object and its (shallow) clone, we see what we'd expect:

```
>>> a
Point(23, 42)
>>> b
Point(23, 42)
>>> a is b
False
```

Here's something else to keep in mind. Because our point object uses primitive types (ints) for its coordinates, there's no difference between a shallow and a deep copy in this case. But I'll expand the example in a second.

Let's move on to a more complex example. I'm going to define another class to represent 2D rectangles. I'll do it in a way that allows us to create a more complex object hierarchy—my rectangles will use Point objects to represent their coordinates:

```
class Rectangle:
    def __init__(self, topleft, bottomright):
        self.topleft = topleft
        self.bottomright = bottomright

    def __repr__(self):
        return (f'Rectangle({self.topleft!r}, '
                f'{self.bottomright!r})')
```

Again, first we're going to attempt to create a shallow copy of a rectangle instance:

```
rect = Rectangle(Point(0, 1), Point(5, 6))
srect = copy.copy(rect)
```

If you inspect the original rectangle and its copy, you'll see how nicely the __repr__() override is working out, and that the shallow copy process worked as expected:

```
>>> rect
Rectangle(Point(0, 1), Point(5, 6))
>>> srect
Rectangle(Point(0, 1), Point(5, 6))
>>> rect is srect
False
```

Remember how the previous list example illustrated the difference between deep and shallow copies? I'm going to use the same approach here. I'll modify an object deeper in the object hierarchy, and then you'll see this change reflected in the (shallow) copy as well:

```
>>> rect.topleft.x = 999
>>> rect
Rectangle(Point(999, 1), Point(5, 6))
>>> srect
Rectangle(Point(999, 1), Point(5, 6))
```

I hope this behaved how you expected it to. Next, I'll create a deep copy of the original rectangle. Then I'll apply another modification and you'll see which objects are affected:

```
>>> drect = copy.deepcopy(srect)
>>> drect.topleft.x = 222
>>> drect
Rectangle(Point(222, 1), Point(5, 6))
>>> rect
```

```
Rectangle(Point(999, 1), Point(5, 6))
>>> srect
Rectangle(Point(999, 1), Point(5, 6))
```

Voila! This time the deep copy (drect) is fully independent of the original (rect) and the shallow copy (srect).

We've covered a lot of ground here, and there are still some finer points to copying objects.

It pays to go deep (ha!) on this topic, so you may want to study up on the copy module documentation.[3] For example, objects can control how they're copied by defining the special methods __copy__() and __deepcopy__() on them. Have fun!

Key Takeaways

- Making a shallow copy of an object won't clone child objects. Therefore, the copy is not fully independent of the original.
- A deep copy of an object will recursively clone child objects. The clone is fully independent of the original, but creating a deep copy is slower.
- You can copy arbitrary objects (including custom classes) with the copy module.

---

[3]cf. Python docs: "Shallow and deep copy operations"

4.5 Abstract Base Classes Keep Inheritance in Check

Abstract Base Classes (ABCs) ensure that derived classes implement particular methods from the base class. In this chapter you'll learn about the benefits of abstract base classes and how to define them with Python's built-in abc module.

So what are Abstract Base Classes good for? A while ago I had a discussion at work about which pattern to use for implementing a maintainable class hierarchy in Python. More specifically, the goal was to define a simple class hierarchy for a service backend in the most programmer-friendly and maintainable way.

We had a `BaseService` class that defined a common interface and several concrete implementations. The concrete implementations do different things but all of them provide the same interface (`MockService`, `RealService`, and so on). To make this relationship explicit, the concrete implementations all subclass `BaseService`.

To make this code as maintainable and programmer-friendly as possible we wanted to make sure that:

- instantiating the base class is impossible; and
- forgetting to implement interface methods in one of the subclasses raises an error as early as possible.

Now why would you want to use Python's abc module to solve this problem? The above design is pretty common in more complex systems. To enforce that a derived class implements a number of methods from the base class, something like this Python idiom is typically used:

```python
class Base:
    def foo(self):
        raise NotImplementedError()
```

```python
    def bar(self):
        raise NotImplementedError()

class Concrete(Base):
    def foo(self):
        return 'foo() called'

    # Oh no, we forgot to override bar()...
    # def bar(self):
    #     return "bar() called"
```

So, what do we get from this first attempt at solving the problem? Calling methods on an instance of Base correctly raises NotImplementedError exceptions:

```python
>>> b = Base()
>>> b.foo()
NotImplementedError
```

Furthermore, instantiating and using Concrete works as expected. And, if we call an unimplemented method like bar() on it, this also raises an exception:

```python
>>> c = Concrete()
>>> c.foo()
'foo() called'
>>> c.bar()
NotImplementedError
```

This first implementation is decent, but it isn't perfect yet. The downsides here are that we can still:

- instantiate Base just fine without getting an error; and

- provide incomplete subclasses—instantiating `Concrete` will not raise an error until we call the missing method `bar()`.

With Python's abc module that was added in Python 2.6,[4] we can do better and solve these remaining issues. Here's an updated implementation using an Abstract Base Class defined with the abc module:

```python
from abc import ABCMeta, abstractmethod

class Base(metaclass=ABCMeta):
    @abstractmethod
    def foo(self):
        pass

    @abstractmethod
    def bar(self):
        pass

class Concrete(Base):
    def foo(self):
        pass

    # We forget to declare bar() again...
```

This still behaves as expected and creates the correct class hierarchy:

```python
assert issubclass(Concrete, Base)
```

Yet, we do get another very useful benefit here. Subclasses of `Base` raise a `TypeError` *at instantiation time* whenever we forget to implement any abstract methods. The raised exception tells us which method or methods we're missing:

---

[4]cf. Python Docs: abc module

```
>>> c = Concrete()
TypeError:
"Can't instantiate abstract class Concrete
with abstract methods bar"
```

Without abc, we'd only get a NotImplementedError if a missing method was actually called. Being notified about missing methods at instantiation time is a great advantage. It makes it more difficult to write invalid subclasses. This might not be a big deal if you're writing new code, but a few weeks or months down the line, I promise it'll be helpful.

This pattern is not a full replacement for compile-time type checking, of course. However, I found it often makes my class hierarchies more robust and more readily maintainable. Using ABCs states the programmer's intent clearly and thus makes the code more communicative. I'd encourage you to read the abc module documentation and to keep an eye out for situations where applying this pattern makes sense.

Key Takeaways

- Abstract Base Classes (ABCs) ensure that derived classes implement particular methods from the base class at instantiation time.
- Using ABCs can help avoid bugs and make class hierarchies easier to maintain.

4.6 What Namedtuples Are Good For

Python comes with a specialized "namedtuple" container type that doesn't seem to get the attention it deserves. It's one of those amazing features in Python that's hidden in plain sight.

Namedtuples can be a great alternative to defining a class manually, and they have some other interesting features that I want to introduce you to in this chapter.

Now, what's a namedtuple and what makes it so special? A good way to think about namedtuples is to view them as an extension of the built-in `tuple` data type.

Python's tuples are a simple data structure for grouping arbitrary objects. Tuples are also immutable—they cannot be modified once they've been created. Here's a brief example:

```
>>> tup = ('hello', object(), 42)
>>> tup
('hello', <object object at 0x105e76b70>, 42)
>>> tup[2]
42
>>> tup[2] = 23
TypeError:
"'tuple' object does not support item assignment"
```

One downside of plain tuples is that the data you store in them can only be pulled out by accessing it through integer indexes. You can't give names to individual properties stored in a tuple. This can impact code readability.

Also, a tuple is always an ad-hoc structure. It's hard to ensure that two tuples have the same number of fields and the same properties stored on them. This makes it easy to introduce "slip-of-the-mind" bugs by mixing up the field order.

Namedtuples to the Rescue

Namedtuples aim to solve these two problems.

First of all, namedtuples are immutable containers, just like regular tuples. Once you store data in top-level attribute on a namedtuple, you can't modify it by updating the attribute. All attributes on a namedtuple object follow the "write once, read many" principle.

Besides that, namedtuples are, well...*named tuples*. Each object stored in them can be accessed through a unique (human-readable) identifier. This frees you from having to remember integer indexes, or resorting to workarounds like defining integer constants as mnemonics for your indexes.

Here's what a namedtuple looks like:

```
>>> from collections import namedtuple
>>> Car = namedtuple('Car' , 'color mileage')
```

Namedtuples were added to the standard library in Python 2.6. To use them, you need to import the `collections` module. In the above example, I defined a simple `Car` data type with two fields: `color` and `mileage`.

You might be wondering why I'm passing the string `'Car'` as the first argument to the `namedtuple` factory function in this example.

This parameter is referred to as the "typename" in the Python docs. It's the name of the new class that's being created by calling the `namedtuple` function.

Since `namedtuple` has no way of knowing what the name of the variable is we're assigning the resulting class to, we need to explicitly tell it which class name we want to use. The class name is used in the docstring and the __repr__ implementation that `namedtuple` automatically generates for us.

And there's another syntactic oddity in this example—why are we passing the fields as a string that encodes their names as `'color mileage'`?

The answer is that namedtuple's factory function calls `split()` on the field names string to parse it into a list of field names. So this is really just a shorthand for the following two steps:

```
>>> 'color mileage'.split()
['color', 'mileage']
>>> Car = namedtuple('Car', ['color', 'mileage'])
```

Of course, you can also pass in a list with string field names directly if you prefer how that looks. The advantage of using a proper list is that it's easier to reformat this code if you need to split it across multiple lines:

```
>>> Car = namedtuple('Car', [
...         'color',
...         'mileage',
... ])
```

Whatever you decide, you can now create new "car" objects with the Car factory function. It behaves as if you had defined a Car class manually and given it a constructor accepting a "color" and a "mileage" value:

```
>>> my_car = Car('red', 3812.4)
>>> my_car.color
'red'
>>> my_car.mileage
3812.4
```

Besides accessing the values stored in a namedtuple by their identifiers, you can still access them by their index. That way, namedtuples can be used as a drop-in replacement for regular tuples:

```
>>> my_car[0]
'red'
>>> tuple(my_car)
('red', 3812.4)
```

Tuple unpacking and the *-operator for function argument unpacking also work as expected:

```
>>> color, mileage = my_car
>>> print(color, mileage)
red 3812.4
>>> print(*my_car)
red 3812.4
```

You'll even get a nice string representation for your namedtuple object for free, which saves some typing and verbosity:

```
>>> my_car
Car(color='red' , mileage=3812.4)
```

Like tuples, namedtuples are immutable. When you try to overwrite one of their fields, you'll get an `AttributeError` exception:

```
>>> my_car.color = 'blue'
AttributeError: "can't set attribute"
```

Namedtuple objects are implemented as regular Python classes internally. When it comes to memory usage, they are also "better" than regular classes and just as memory efficient as regular tuples.

A good way to view them is to think that *namedtuples are a memory-efficient shortcut to defining an immutable class in Python manually.*

Subclassing Namedtuples

Since they are built on top of regular Python classes, you can even add methods to a namedtuple object. For example, you can extend a namedtuple's class like any other class and add methods and new properties to it that way. Here's an example:

```python
Car = namedtuple('Car', 'color mileage')

class MyCarWithMethods(Car):
    def hexcolor(self):
        if self.color == 'red':
            return '#ff0000'
        else:
            return '#000000'
```

We can now create `MyCarWithMethods` objects and call their `hexcolor()` method, just as expected:

```python
>>> c = MyCarWithMethods('red', 1234)
>>> c.hexcolor()
'#ff0000'
```

However, this might be a little clunky. It might be worth doing if you want a class with immutable properties, but it's also easy to shoot yourself in the foot here.

For example, adding a new *immutable* field is tricky because of how namedtuples are structured internally. The easiest way to create hierarchies of namedtuples is to use the base tuple's `_fields` property:

```python
>>> Car = namedtuple('Car', 'color mileage')
>>> ElectricCar = namedtuple(
...     'ElectricCar', Car._fields + ('charge',))
```

This gives the desired result:

```
>>> ElectricCar('red', 1234, 45.0)
ElectricCar(color='red', mileage=1234, charge=45.0)
```

Built-in Helper Methods

Besides the _fields property, each namedtuple instance also provides a few more helper methods you might find useful. Their names
all start with a single underscore character (_) which usually signals
that a method or property is "private" and not part of the stable public
interface of a class or module.

With namedtuples, the underscore naming convention has a different
meaning though. These helper methods and properties *are* part of
namedtuple's public interface. The helpers were named that way to
avoid naming collisions with user-defined tuple fields. So go ahead
and use them if you need them!

I want to show you a few scenarios where the namedtuple helper
methods might come in handy. Let's start with the _asdict() helper
method. It returns the contents of a namedtuple as a dictionary:

```
>>> my_car._asdict()
OrderedDict([('color', 'red'), ('mileage', 3812.4)])
```

This is great for avoiding typos in the field names when generating
JSON-output, for example:

```
>>> json.dumps(my_car._asdict())
'{"color": "red", "mileage": 3812.4}'
```

Another useful helper is the _replace() function. It creates a (shallow) copy of a tuple and allows you to selectively replace some of its
fields:

```
>>> my_car._replace(color='blue')
Car(color='blue', mileage=3812.4)
```

Lastly, the _make() classmethod can be used to create new instances of a namedtuple from a sequence or iterable:

```
>>> Car._make(['red', 999])
Car(color='red', mileage=999)
```

When to Use Namedtuples

Namedtuples can be an easy way to clean up your code and to make it more readable by enforcing a better structure for your data.

For example, I find that going from ad-hoc data types like dictionaries with a fixed format to namedtuples helps me express my intentions more clearly. Often when I attempt this refactoring I magically come up with a better solution for the problem I'm facing.

Using namedtuples over unstructured tuples and dicts can also make my coworkers' lives easier because they make the data being passed around "self-documenting" (to a degree).

On the other hand, I try not to use namedtuples for their own sake if they don't help me write "cleaner" and more maintainable code. Like many other techniques shown in this book, sometimes there can be *too much of a good thing*.

However, if you use them with care, namedtuples can undoubtedly make your Python code better and more expressive.

Key Takeaways

- `collection.namedtuple` is a memory-efficient shortcut to manually define an immutable class in Python.
- Namedtuples can help clean up your code by enforcing an easier-to-understand structure on your data.

- Namedtuples provide a few useful helper methods that all start with a single underscore, but are part of the public interface. It's okay to use them.

4.7 Class vs Instance Variable Pitfalls

Besides making a distinction between class methods and instance methods, Python's object model also distinguishes between class and instances *variables*.

It's an important distinction, but also one that caused me trouble as a new Python developer. For a long time I didn't invest the time needed to understand these concepts from the ground up. And so my early OOP experiments were riddled with surprising behaviors and odd bugs. In this chapter we'll clear up any lingering confusion about this topic with some hands-on examples.

Like I said, there are two kinds of data attributes on Python objects: *class variables* and *instance variables*.

Class variables are declared inside the class definition (but outside of any instance methods). They're not tied to any particular instance of a class. Instead, class variables store their contents on the class itself, and all objects created from a particular class share access to the same set of class variables. This means, for example, that modifying a class variable affects all object instances at the same time.

Instance variables are always tied to a particular object instance. Their contents are not stored on the class, but on each individual object created from the class. Therefore, the contents of an instance variable are completely independent from one object instance to the next. And so, modifying an instance variable only affects one object instance at a time.

Okay, this was fairly abstract—time to look at some code! Let's bust out the old "dog example"... For some reason, OOP-tutorials always use cars or pets to illustrate their point, and it's hard to break with that tradition.

What does a happy dog need? Four legs and a name:

```
class Dog:
    num_legs = 4   # <- Class variable

    def __init__(self, name):
        self.name = name   # <- Instance variable
```

Alright, that's a neat object-oriented representation of the dog situation I just described. Creating new Dog instances works as expected, and they each get an instance variable called name:

```
>>> jack = Dog('Jack')
>>> jill = Dog('Jill')
>>> jack.name, jill.name
('Jack', 'Jill')
```

There's a little more flexibility when it comes to class variables. You can access the num_legs class variable either directly on each Dog instance or *on the class itself*:

```
>>> jack.num_legs, jill.num_legs
(4, 4)
>>> Dog.num_legs
4
```

However, if you try to access an *instance* variable through the class, it'll fail with an AttributeError. Instance variables are specific to each object instance and are created when the __init__ constructor runs—they don't even exist on the class itself.

This is the central distinction between class and instance variables:

```
>>> Dog.name
AttributeError:
"type object 'Dog' has no attribute 'name'"
```

Alright, so far so good.

Let's say that Jack the Dog gets a little too close to the microwave when he eats his dinner one day—and he sprouts an extra pair of legs. How'd you represent that in the little code sandbox we've got so far?

The first idea for a solution might be to simply modify the num_legs variable on the Dog class:

```
>>> Dog.num_legs = 6
```

But remember, we don't want *all* dogs to start scurrying around on six legs. So now we've just turned every dog instance in our little universe into Super Dog because we've modified a *class* variable. And this affects all dogs, even those created previously:

```
>>> jack.num_legs, jill.num_legs
(6, 6)
```

So that didn't work. The reason it didn't work is that modifying a class variable *on the class namespace* affects all instances of the class. Let's roll back the change to the class variable and instead try to give an extra pair o' legs specifically to Jack only:

```
>>> Dog.num_legs = 4
>>> jack.num_legs = 6
```

Now, what monstrosities did this create? Let's find out:

```
>>> jack.num_legs, jill.num_legs, Dog.num_legs
(6, 4, 4)
```

Okay, this looks "pretty good" (aside from the fact that we just gave poor Jack some extra legs). But how did this change actually affect our Dog objects?

You see, the trouble here is that while we got the result we wanted (extra legs for Jack), we introduced a num_legs instance variable to the Jack instance. And now the new num_legs instance variable "shadows" the class variable of the same name, overriding and hiding it when we access the object instance scope:

```
>>> jack.num_legs, jack.__class__.num_legs
(6, 4)
```

As you can see, the class variables seemingly got *out of sync*. This happened because writing to jack.num_legs created an *instance variable* with the same name as the class variable.

This isn't necessarily bad, but it's important to be aware of what happened here, behind the scenes. Before I finally understood class-level and instance-level scope in Python, this was a great avenue for bugs to slip into my programs.

To tell you the truth, trying to modify a class variable through an object instance—which then accidentally creates an instance variable of the same name, shadowing the original class variable—is a bit of an OOP pitfall in Python.

A Dog-free Example

While no dogs were harmed in the making of this chapter (it's all fun and games until someone sprouts and extra pair of legs), I wanted to give you one more practical example of the useful things you can do with class variables. Something that's a little closer to the real-world applications for class variables.

So here it is. The following CountedObject class keeps track of how many times it was instantiated over the lifetime of a program (which might actually be an interesting performance metric to know):

```
class CountedObject:
    num_instances = 0

    def __init__(self):
        self.__class__.num_instances += 1
```

CountedObject keeps a num_instances class variable that serves as a shared counter. When the class is declared, it initializes the counter to zero and then leaves it alone.

Every time you create a new instance of this class, it increments the shared counter by one when the __init__ constructor runs:

```
>>> CountedObject.num_instances
0
>>> CountedObject().num_instances
1
>>> CountedObject().num_instances
2
>>> CountedObject().num_instances
3
>>> CountedObject.num_instances
3
```

Notice how this code needs to jump through a little hoop to make sure it increments the counter variable *on the class*. It would've been an easy mistake to make if I had written the constructor as follows:

```
# WARNING: This implementation contains a bug

class BuggyCountedObject:
    num_instances = 0

    def __init__(self):
        self.num_instances += 1  # !!!
```

As you'll see, this (bad) implementation never increments the shared counter variable:

```
>>> BuggyCountedObject.num_instances
0
>>> BuggyCountedObject().num_instances
1
>>> BuggyCountedObject().num_instances
1
>>> BuggyCountedObject().num_instances
1
>>> BuggyCountedObject.num_instances
0
```

I'm sure you can see where I went wrong now. This (buggy) implementation never increments the shared counter because I made the mistake I explained in the "Jack the Dog" example earlier. This implementation won't work because I accidentally "shadowed" the num_instance class variable by creating an instance variable of the same name in the constructor.

It correctly calculates the new value for the counter (going from 0 to 1), but then stores the result in an instance variable—which means other instances of the class never even see the updated counter value.

As you can see, that's quite an easy mistake to make. It's a good idea to be careful and double-check your scoping when dealing with shared state on a class. Automated tests and peer reviews help greatly with that.

Nevertheless, I hope you can see why and how class variables—despite their pitfalls—can be useful tools in practice. Good luck!

Key Takeaways

- Class variables are for data shared by all instances of a class. They belong to a class, not a specific instance and are shared among all instances of a class.

- Instance variables are for data that is unique to each instance. They belong to individual object instances and are not shared among the other instances of a class. Each instance variable gets a unique backing store specific to the instance.
- Because class variables can be "shadowed" by instance variables of the same name, it's easy to (accidentally) override class variables in a way that introduces bugs and odd behavior.

4.8 Instance, Class, and Static Methods Demystified

In this chapter you'll see what's behind *class methods*, *static methods*, and regular *instance methods* in Python.

If you develop an intuitive understanding for their differences, you'll be able to write object-oriented Python that communicates its intent more clearly and will be easier to maintain in the long run.

Let's begin by writing a (Python 3) class that contains simple examples for all three method types:

```python
class MyClass:
    def method(self):
        return 'instance method called', self

    @classmethod
    def classmethod(cls):
        return 'class method called', cls

    @staticmethod
    def staticmethod():
        return 'static method called'
```

Note for Python 2 users: The `@staticmethod` and `@classmethod` decorators are available as of Python 2.4 and so this example will work as is. Instead of using a plain `class MyClass` declaration, you might choose to declare a new-style class inheriting from `object` with the `class MyClass(object)` syntax. But other than that, you're golden!

Instance Methods

The first method on `MyClass`, called `method`, is a regular *instance method*. That's the basic, no-frills method type you'll use most of the time. You can see the method takes one parameter, `self`, which

145

points to an instance of `MyClass` when the method is called. But of course, instance methods can accept more than just one parameter.

Through the `self` parameter, instance methods can freely access attributes and other methods on the same object. This gives them a lot of power when it comes to modifying an object's state.

Not only can they modify object state, instance methods can also access the class itself through the `self.__class__` attribute. This means instance methods can also modify class state.

Class Methods

Let's compare that to the second method, `MyClass.classmethod`. I marked this method with a `@classmethod`[5] decorator to flag it as a *class method*.

Instead of accepting a `self` parameter, class methods take a `cls` parameter that points to the class—and not the object instance—when the method is called.

Since the class method only has access to this `cls` argument, it can't modify object instance state. That would require access to `self`. However, class methods can still modify class state that applies across all instances of the class.

Static Methods

The third method, `MyClass.staticmethod` was marked with a `@staticmethod`[6] decorator to flag it as a *static method*.

This type of method doesn't take a `self` or a `cls` parameter, although, of course, it can be made to accept an arbitrary number of other parameters.

---

[5]cf. Python Docs: "@classmethod"
[6]cf. Python Docs: "@staticmethod"

As a result, a static method cannot modify object state or class state. Static methods are restricted in what data they can access—they're primarily a way to namespace your methods.

Let's See Them in Action!

I know this discussion has been fairly theoretical up to this point. I also believe it's important that you develop an intuitive understanding for how these method types differ in practice. That's why we'll go over some concrete examples now.

Let's take a look at how these methods behave in action when we call them. We'll start by creating an instance of the class and then calling the three different methods on it.

MyClass was set up in such a way that each method's implementation returns a tuple containing information we can use to trace what's going on and which parts of the class or object that method can access.

Here's what happens when we call an **instance method**:

```
>>> obj = MyClass()
>>> obj.method()
('instance method called', <MyClass instance at 0x11a2>)
```

This confirms that, in this case, the instance method called method has access to the object instance (printed as <MyClass instance>) via the self argument.

When the method is called, Python replaces the self argument with the instance object, obj. We could ignore the syntactic sugar provided by the obj.method() dot-call syntax and pass the instance object *manually* to get the same result:

```
>>> MyClass.method(obj)
('instance method called', <MyClass instance at 0x11a2>)
```

By the way, instance methods can also access the *class itself* through the self.__class__ attribute. This makes instance methods powerful in terms of access restrictions—they can freely modify state on the object instance *and* on the class itself.

Let's try out the **class method** next:

```
>>> obj.classmethod()
('class method called', <class MyClass at 0x11a2>)
```

Calling classmethod() showed us that it doesn't have access to the <MyClass instance> object, but only to the <class MyClass> object, representing the class itself (everything in Python is an object, even classes themselves).

Notice how Python automatically passes the class as the first argument to the function when we call MyClass.classmethod(). Calling a method in Python through the *dot syntax* triggers this behavior. The self parameter on instance methods works the same way.

Please note that naming these parameters self and cls is just a convention. You could just as easily name them the_object and the_class and get the same result. All that matters is that they're positioned first in the parameter list for that particular method.

Time to call the **static method** now:

```
>>> obj.staticmethod()
'static method called'
```

Did you see how we called staticmethod() on the object and were able to do so successfully? Some developers are surprised when they learn that it's possible to call a static method on an object instance.

Behind the scenes, Python simply enforces the access restrictions by not passing in the self or the cls argument when a static method gets called using the dot syntax.

This confirms that static methods can neither access the object instance state nor the class state. They work like regular functions but belong to the class' (and every instance's) namespace.

Now, let's take a look at what happens when we attempt to call these methods on the class itself, without creating an object instance beforehand:

```
>>> MyClass.classmethod()
('class method called', <class MyClass at 0x11a2>)

>>> MyClass.staticmethod()
'static method called'

>>> MyClass.method()
TypeError: """unbound method method() must
    be called with MyClass instance as first
    argument (got nothing instead)"""
```

We were able to call `classmethod()` and `staticmethod()` just fine, but attempting to call the instance method `method()` failed with a `TypeError`.

This is to be expected. This time we didn't create an object instance and tried calling an instance function directly on the class blueprint itself. This means there is no way for Python to populate the `self` argument and therefore the call fails with a `TypeError` exception.

This should make the distinction between these three method types a little more clear. But don't worry, I'm not going to leave it at that. In the next two sections I'll go over two slightly more realistic examples of when to use these special method types.

I will base my examples around this bare-bones `Pizza` class:

```
class Pizza:
    def __init__(self, ingredients):
        self.ingredients = ingredients

    def __repr__(self):
        return f'Pizza({self.ingredients!r})'

>>> Pizza(['cheese', 'tomatoes'])
Pizza(['cheese', 'tomatoes'])
```

Delicious Pizza Factories With @classmethod

If you've had any exposure to pizza in the real world, you'll know that there are many delicious variations available:

```
Pizza(['mozzarella', 'tomatoes'])
Pizza(['mozzarella', 'tomatoes', 'ham', 'mushrooms'])
Pizza(['mozzarella'] * 4)
```

The Italians figured out their pizza taxonomy centuries ago, and so these delicious types of pizza all have their own names. We'd do well to take advantage of that and give the users of our Pizza class a better interface for creating the pizza objects they crave.

A nice and clean way to do that is by using class methods as *factory functions*[7] for the different kinds of pizzas we can create:

```
class Pizza:
    def __init__(self, ingredients):
        self.ingredients = ingredients

    def __repr__(self):
        return f'Pizza({self.ingredients!r})'
```

---

[7]cf. Wikipedia: "Factory (object-oriented programming)"

```
@classmethod
def margherita(cls):
    return cls(['mozzarella', 'tomatoes'])

@classmethod
def prosciutto(cls):
    return cls(['mozzarella', 'tomatoes', 'ham'])
```

Note how I'm using the cls argument in the margherita and prosciutto factory methods instead of calling the Pizza constructor directly.

This is a trick you can use to follow the *Don't Repeat Yourself (DRY)*[8] principle. If we decide to rename this class at some point, we won't have to remember to update the constructor name in all of the factory functions.

Now, what can we do with these factory methods? Let's try them out:

```
>>> Pizza.margherita()
Pizza(['mozzarella', 'tomatoes'])

>>> Pizza.prosciutto()
Pizza(['mozzarella', 'tomatoes', 'ham'])
```

As you can see, we can use the factory functions to create new Pizza objects that are configured just the way we want them. They all use the same __init__ constructor internally and simply provide a shortcut for remembering all of the various ingredients.

Another way to look at this use of class methods is to realize that they allow you to define alternative constructors for your classes.

Python only allows one __init__ method per class. Using class methods makes it possible to add as many alternative constructors as nec-

---

[8]cf. Wikipedia: "Don't repeat yourself"

essary. This can make the interface for your classes self-documenting (to a certain degree) and simplify their usage.

When To Use Static Methods

It's a little more difficult to come up with a good example here, but tell you what—I'll just keep stretching the pizza analogy thinner and thinner... (yum!)

Here's what I came up with:

```python
import math

class Pizza:
    def __init__(self, radius, ingredients):
        self.radius = radius
        self.ingredients = ingredients

    def __repr__(self):
        return (f'Pizza({self.radius!r}, '
                f'{self.ingredients!r})')

    def area(self):
        return self.circle_area(self.radius)

    @staticmethod
    def circle_area(r):
        return r ** 2 * math.pi
```

Now what did I change here? First, I modified the constructor and __repr__ to accept an extra radius argument.

I also added an area() instance method that calculates and returns the pizza's area. This would also be a good candidate for an @property—but hey, this is just a toy example.

Instead of calculating the area directly within area(), by using the well-known circle area formula, I factored that out to a separate circle_area() static method.

Let's try it out!

```
>>> p = Pizza(4, ['mozzarella', 'tomatoes'])
>>> p
Pizza(4, {self.ingredients})
>>> p.area()
50.26548245743669
>>> Pizza.circle_area(4)
50.26548245743669
```

Sure, this is still a bit of a simplistic example, but it'll help explain some of the benefits that static methods provide.

As we've learned, static methods can't access class or instance state because they don't take a cls or self argument. That's a big limitation—but it's also a great signal to show that a particular method is independent from everything else around it.

In the above example, it's clear that circle_area() can't modify the class or the class instance in any way. (Sure, you could always work around that with a global variable, but that's not the point here.)

Now, why is that useful?

Flagging a method as a static method is not just a hint that a method won't modify class or instance state. As you've seen, this restriction is also enforced by the Python runtime.

Techniques like that allow you to communicate clearly about parts of your class architecture so that new development work is naturally guided to happen within these boundaries. Of course, it would be easy enough to defy these restrictions. But in practice, they often help avoid accidental modifications that go against the original design.

Put differently, using static methods and class methods are ways to communicate developer intent while enforcing that intent enough to avoid most "slip of the mind" mistakes and bugs that would break the design.

Applied sparingly and when it makes sense, writing some of your methods that way can provide maintenance benefits and make it less likely that other developers use your classes incorrectly.

Static methods also have benefits when it comes to writing test code. Since the `circle_area()` method is completely independent from the rest of the class, it's much easier to test.

We don't have to worry about setting up a complete class instance before we can test the method in a unit test. We can just fire away like we would if we were testing a regular function. Again, this makes future maintenance easier and provides a link between object-oriented and procedural programming styles.

Key Takeaways

- Instance methods need a class instance and can access the instance through `self`.
- Class methods don't need a class instance. They can't access the instance (`self`) but they have access to the class itself via `cls`.
- Static methods don't have access to `cls` or `self`. They work like regular functions but belong to the class' namespace.
- Static and class methods communicate and (to a certain degree) enforce developer intent about class design. This can have definite maintenance benefits.

Chapter 5

Common Data Structures in Python

What's something that every Python developer should practice and learn more about?

Data structures. They're the fundamental constructs around which you build your programs. Each data structure provides a particular way of organizing data so it can be accessed efficiently, depending on your use case.

I believe that going back to the fundamentals always pays off for a programmer, regardless of their skill level or experience.

Now, I don't advocate that you should focus on expanding your data structures knowledge alone—the "failure mode" for that is getting stuck in theory la-la land and never shipping anything...

But I found that spending *some* time on brushing up your data structures (and algorithms) knowledge *always* pays off.

Whether you do that with a tightly focused "sprint" for a few days, or as an ongoing project with little pockets of time here and there doesn't really matter. Either way, I promise it'll be time well spent.

Alright, so data structures in Python, eh? We've got lists, dicts, sets...umm. Stacks? Do we have stacks?

You see, the trouble is that Python ships with an extensive set of data structures in its standard library. However, sometimes the naming for them is a bit "off".

It's often unclear how even well-known "abstract data types" like a Stack correspond to a specific implementation in Python. Other languages like Java stick to a more "computer-sciency" and explicit naming scheme: A list isn't just a "list" in Java—it's either a `LinkedList` or an `ArrayList`.

This makes it easier to recognize the expected behavior and the computational complexity of these types. Python favors a simpler and more "human" naming scheme, and I love it. In part, it's what makes programming with Python so much fun.

But the downside is that even to experienced Python developers, it can be unclear whether the built-in `list` type is implemented as a linked list or a dynamic array. And the day will come when lacking this knowledge will cause them endless hours of frustration, or get them rejected in a job interview.

In this part of the book you'll take a tour of the fundamental data structures and implementations of abstract data types (ADTs) built into Python and its standard library.

My goal here is to clarify how the most common abstract data types map to Python's naming scheme and to provide a brief description for each. This information will also help you shine in Python coding interviews.

If you're looking for a good book to brush up on your general data structures knowledge, I highly recommend Steven S. Skiena's *The Algorithm Design Manual*.

It strikes a great balance between teaching you fundamental (and more advanced) data structures, and then showing you how to put them to practical use in various algorithms. Steve's book was a great help in the writing of these chapters.

5.1 Dictionaries, Maps, and Hashtables

In Python, dictionaries (or "dicts" for short) are a central data structure. Dicts store an arbitrary number of objects, each identified by a unique dictionary *key*.

Dictionaries are also often called *maps*, *hashmaps*, *lookup tables*, or *associative arrays*. They allow for the efficient lookup, insertion, and deletion of any object associated with a given key.

What does this mean in practice? It turns out that *phone books* make a decent real-world analog for dictionary objects:

> *Phone books allow you to quickly retrieve the information (phone number) associated with a given key (a person's name). So, instead of having to read a phone book front to back in order to find someone's number, you can jump more or less directly to a name and look up the associated information.*

This analogy breaks down somewhat when it comes to *how* the information is organized in order to allow for fast lookups. But the fundamental performance characteristics hold: Dictionaries allow you to quickly find the information associated with a given key.

In summary, dictionaries are one of the most frequently used and most important data structures in computer science.

So, how does Python handle dictionaries?

Let's take a tour of the dictionary implementations available in core Python and the Python standard library.

dict – Your Go-To Dictionary

Because of their importance, Python features a robust dictionary implementation that's built directly into the core language: the dict data type.[1]

Python also provides some useful "syntactic sugar" for working with dictionaries in your programs. For example, the curly-braces dictionary expression syntax and dictionary comprehensions allow you to conveniently define new dictionary objects:

```python
phonebook = {
    'bob': 7387,
    'alice': 3719,
    'jack': 7052,
}

squares = {x: x * x for x in range(6)}

>>> phonebook['alice']
3719

>>> squares
{0: 0, 1: 1, 2: 4, 3: 9, 4: 16, 5: 25}
```

There are some restrictions on which objects can be used as valid keys.

Python's dictionaries are indexed by keys that can be of any hashable type[2]: A hashable object has a hash value which never changes during its lifetime (see __hash__), and it can be compared to other objects (see __eq__). In addition, hashable objects which compare as equal must have the same hash value.

Immutable types like strings and numbers are hashable and work well as dictionary keys. You can also use tuple objects as dictionary keys, as long as they contain only hashable types themselves.

For most use cases, Python's built-in dictionary implementation will do everything you need. Dictionaries are highly optimized and un-

---

[1]cf. Python Docs: "Mapping Types — dict"
[2]cf. Python Docs Glossary: "Hashable"

derlie many parts of the language, for example class attributes and variables in a stack frame are both stored internally in dictionaries.

Python dictionaries are based on a well-tested and finely tuned hash table implementation that provides the performance characteristics you'd expect: $O(1)$ time complexity for lookup, insert, update, and delete operations in the average case.

There's little reason not to use the standard dict implementation included with Python. However, specialized third-party dictionary implementations exist, for example skip lists or B-tree based dictionaries.

Besides "plain" dict objects, Python's standard library also includes a number of specialized dictionary implementations. These specialized dictionaries are all based on the built-in dictionary class (and share its performance characteristics), but add some convenience features on top of that.

Let's take a look at them.

collections.OrderedDict – Remember the Insertion Order of Keys

Python includes a specialized dict subclass that remembers the insertion order of keys added to it: collections.OrderedDict.[3]

While standard dict instances preserve the insertion order of keys in CPython 3.6 and above, this is just a side effect of the CPython implementation and is not defined in the language spec.[4] So, if key order is important for your algorithm to work, it's best to communicate this clearly by explicitly using the OrderDict class.

By the way, OrderedDict is not a built-in part of the core language and must be imported from the collections module in the standard library.

---

[3]cf. Python Docs: "collections.OrderedDict"
[4]cf. CPython mailing list

```
>>> import collections
>>> d = collections.OrderedDict(one=1, two=2, three=3)

>>> d
OrderedDict([('one', 1), ('two', 2), ('three', 3)])

>>> d['four'] = 4
>>> d
OrderedDict([('one', 1), ('two', 2),
            ('three', 3), ('four', 4)])

>>> d.keys()
odict_keys(['one', 'two', 'three', 'four'])
```

collections.defaultdict – Return Default Values for Missing Keys

The defaultdict class is another dictionary subclass that accepts a callable in its constructor whose return value will be used if a requested key cannot be found.[5]

This can save you some typing and make the programmer's intentions more clear, as compared to using the get() methods or catching a KeyError exception in regular dictionaries.

```
>>> from collections import defaultdict
>>> dd = defaultdict(list)

# Accessing a missing key creates it and
# initializes it using the default factory,
# i.e. list() in this example:
>>> dd['dogs'].append('Rufus')
>>> dd['dogs'].append('Kathrin')
>>> dd['dogs'].append('Mr Sniffles')
```

---

[5]cf. Python Docs: "collections.defaultdict"

```
>>> dd['dogs']
['Rufus', 'Kathrin', 'Mr Sniffles']
```

collections.ChainMap – Search Multiple Dictionaries as a Single Mapping

The collections.ChainMap data structure groups multiple dictionaries into a single mapping.[6] Lookups search the underlying mappings one by one until a key is found. Insertions, updates, and deletions only affect the first mapping added to the chain.

```
>>> from collections import ChainMap
>>> dict1 = {'one': 1, 'two': 2}
>>> dict2 = {'three': 3, 'four': 4}
>>> chain = ChainMap(dict1, dict2)

>>> chain
ChainMap({'one': 1, 'two': 2}, {'three': 3, 'four': 4})

# ChainMap searches each collection in the chain
# from left to right until it finds the key (or fails):
>>> chain['three']
3
>>> chain['one']
1
>>> chain['missing']
KeyError: 'missing'
```

types.MappingProxyType – A Wrapper for Making Read-Only Dictionaries

MappingProxyType is a wrapper around a standard dictionary that provides a read-only view into the wrapped dictionary's data.[7] This

---

[6]cf. Python Docs: "collections.ChainMap"
[7]cf. Python Docs: "types.MappingProxyType"

class was added in Python 3.3, and it can be used to create immutable proxy versions of dictionaries.

For example, this can be helpful if you'd like to return a dictionary carrying internal state from a class or module, while discouraging write access to this object. Using MappingProxyType allows you to put these restrictions in place without first having to create a full copy of the dictionary.

```python
>>> from types import MappingProxyType
>>> writable = {'one': 1, 'two': 2}
>>> read_only = MappingProxyType(writable)

# The proxy is read-only:
>>> read_only['one']
1
>>> read_only['one'] = 23
TypeError:
"'mappingproxy' object does not support item assignment"

# Updates to the original are reflected in the proxy:
>>> writable['one'] = 42
>>> read_only
mappingproxy({'one': 42, 'two': 2})
```

Dictionaries in Python: Conclusion

All of the Python dictionary implementations listed in this chapter are valid implementations that are built into the Python standard library.

If you're looking for a general recommendation on which mapping type to use in your programs, I'd point you to the built-in dict data type. It's a versatile and optimized hash table implementation that's built directly into the core language.

I would only recommend that you use one of the other data types listed here if you have special requirements that go beyond what's provided by `dict`.

Yes, I still believe all of them are valid options—but usually your code will be more clear and easier to maintain by other developers if it relies on standard Python dictionaries most of the time.

Key Takeaways

- Dictionaries are *the* central data structure in Python.
- The built-in `dict` type will be "good enough" most of the time.
- Specialized implementations, like read-only or ordered dicts, are available in the Python standard library.

5.2 Array Data Structures

An array is a fundamental data structure available in most programming languages, and it has a wide range of uses across different algorithms.

In this chapter we'll take a look at array implementations in Python that only use core language features or functionality that's included in the Python standard library.

You'll see the strengths and weaknesses of each approach so you can decide which implementation is right for your use case. But before we jump in, let's cover some of the basics first.

How do arrays work, and what are they used for?

Arrays consist of fixed-size data records that allow each element to be efficiently located based on its index.

Because arrays store information in adjoining blocks of memory, they're considered *contiguous* data structures (as opposed to *linked* datas structure like linked lists, for example.)

A real world analogy for an array data structure is a *parking lot*:

> *You can look at the parking lot as a whole and treat it as a single object, but inside the lot there are parking spots indexed by a unique number. Parking spots are containers for vehicles—each parking spot can either be empty or have a car, a motorbike, or some other vehicle parked on it.*

But not all parking lots are the same:

> *Some parking lots may be restricted to only one type of vehicle. For example, a motor-home parking lot wouldn't allow bikes to be parked on it. A "restricted" parking lot*

corresponds to a "typed array" data structure that only allows elements that have the same data type stored in them.

Performance-wise, it's very fast to look up an element contained in an array given the element's index. A proper array implementation guarantees a constant $O(1)$ access time for this case.

Python includes several array-like data structures in its standard library that each have slightly different characteristics. Let's take a look at them:

`list` – **Mutable Dynamic Arrays**

Lists are a part of the core Python language.[8] Despite their name, Python's lists are implemented as *dynamic arrays* behind the scenes. This means a list allows elements to be added or removed, and the list will automatically adjust the backing store that holds these elements by allocating or releasing memory.

Python lists can hold arbitrary elements—"everything" is an object in Python, including functions. Therefore, you can mix and match different kinds of data types and store them all in a single list.

This can be a powerful feature, but the downside is that supporting multiple data types at the same time means that data is generally less tightly packed. And as a result, the whole structure takes up more space.

```
>>> arr = ['one', 'two', 'three']
>>> arr[0]
'one'

# Lists have a nice repr:
>>> arr
```

---

[8]cf. Python Docs: "list"

```
['one', 'two', 'three']

# Lists are mutable:
>>> arr[1] = 'hello'
>>> arr
['one', 'hello', 'three']

>>> del arr[1]
>>> arr
['one', 'three']

# Lists can hold arbitrary data types:
>>> arr.append(23)
>>> arr
['one', 'three', 23]
```

tuple – Immutable Containers

Just like lists, tuples are also a part of the Python core language.[9] Unlike lists, however, Python's tuple objects are immutable. This means elements can't be added or removed dynamically—all elements in a tuple must be defined at creation time.

Just like lists, tuples can hold elements of arbitrary data types. Having this flexibility is powerful, but again, it also means that data is less tightly packed than it would be in a typed array.

```
>>> arr = 'one', 'two', 'three'
>>> arr[0]
'one'

# Tuples have a nice repr:
>>> arr
('one', 'two', 'three')
```

---

[9]cf. Python Docs: "tuple"

```
# Tuples are immutable:
>>> arr[1] = 'hello'
TypeError:
"'tuple' object does not support item assignment"

>>> del arr[1]
TypeError:
"'tuple' object doesn't support item deletion"

# Tuples can hold arbitrary data types:
# (Adding elements creates a copy of the tuple)
>>> arr + (23,)
('one', 'two', 'three', 23)
```

array.array – Basic Typed Arrays

Python's array module provides space-efficient storage of basic C-style data types like bytes, 32-bit integers, floating point numbers, and so on.

Arrays created with the array.array class are mutable and behave similarly to lists, except for one important difference—they are "typed arrays" constrained to a single data type.[10]

Because of this constraint, array.array objects with many elements are more space-efficient than lists and tuples. The elements stored in them are tightly packed, and this can be useful if you need to store many elements of the same type.

Also, arrays support many of the same methods as regular lists, and you might be able to use them as a "drop-in replacement" without requiring other changes to your application code.

```
>>> import array
>>> arr = array.array('f', (1.0, 1.5, 2.0, 2.5))
```

---

[10]cf. Python Docs: "array.array"

```
>>> arr[1]
1.5

# Arrays have a nice repr:
>>> arr
array('f', [1.0, 1.5, 2.0, 2.5])

# Arrays are mutable:
>>> arr[1] = 23.0
>>> arr
array('f', [1.0, 23.0, 2.0, 2.5])

>>> del arr[1]
>>> arr
array('f', [1.0, 2.0, 2.5])

>>> arr.append(42.0)
>>> arr
array('f', [1.0, 2.0, 2.5, 42.0])

# Arrays are "typed":
>>> arr[1] = 'hello'
TypeError: "must be real number, not str"
```

str – Immutable Arrays of Unicode Characters

Python 3.x uses str objects to store textual data as immutable sequences of Unicode characters.[11] Practically speaking, that means a str is an immutable array of characters. Oddly enough, it's also a recursive data structure—each character in a string is a str object of length 1 itself.

String objects are space-efficient because they're tightly packed and they specialize in a single data type. If you're storing Unicode text, you should use them. Because strings are immutable in Python, modifying

---

[11]cf. Python Docs: "str"

a string requires creating a modified copy. The closest equivalent to a "mutable string" is storing individual characters inside a list.

```
>>> arr = 'abcd'
>>> arr[1]
'b'

>>> arr
'abcd'

# Strings are immutable:
>>> arr[1] = 'e'
TypeError:
"'str' object does not support item assignment"

>>> del arr[1]
TypeError:
"'str' object doesn't support item deletion"

# Strings can be unpacked into a list to
# get a mutable representation:
>>> list('abcd')
['a', 'b', 'c', 'd']
>>> ''.join(list('abcd'))
'abcd'

# Strings are recursive data structures:
>>> type('abc')
"<class 'str'>"
>>> type('abc'[0])
"<class 'str'>"
```

bytes – Immutable Arrays of Single Bytes

Bytes objects are immutable sequences of single bytes (integers in the range of $0 <= x <= 255$).[12] Conceptually, they're similar to `str` objects, and you can also think of them as immutable arrays of bytes.

Like strings, `bytes` have their own literal syntax for creating objects and they're space-efficient. Bytes objects are immutable, but unlike strings, there's a dedicated "mutable byte array" data type called `bytearray` that they can be unpacked into. You'll hear more about that in the next section.

```
>>> arr = bytes((0, 1, 2, 3))
>>> arr[1]
1

# Bytes literals have their own syntax:
>>> arr
b'\x00\x01\x02\x03'
>>> arr = b'\x00\x01\x02\x03'

# Only valid "bytes" are allowed:
>>> bytes((0, 300))
ValueError: "bytes must be in range(0, 256)"

# Bytes are immutable:
>>> arr[1] = 23
TypeError:
"'bytes' object does not support item assignment"

>>> del arr[1]
TypeError:
"'bytes' object doesn't support item deletion"
```

---

[12] cf. Python Docs: "bytes"

bytearray — Mutable Arrays of Single Bytes

The bytearray type is a mutable sequence of integers in the range
0 <= x <= 255.[13] They're closely related to bytes objects with the
main difference being that bytearrays can be modified freely—you can
overwrite elements, remove existing elements, or add new ones. The
bytearray object will grow and shrink accordingly.

Bytearrays can be converted back into immutable bytes objects but
this involves copying the stored data in full—a slow operation taking
$O(n)$ time.

```
>>> arr = bytearray((0, 1, 2, 3))
>>> arr[1]
1

# The bytearray repr:
>>> arr
bytearray(b'\x00\x01\x02\x03')

# Bytearrays are mutable:
>>> arr[1] = 23
>>> arr
bytearray(b'\x00\x17\x02\x03')

>>> arr[1]
23

# Bytearrays can grow and shrink in size:
>>> del arr[1]
>>> arr
bytearray(b'\x00\x02\x03')

>>> arr.append(42)
>>> arr
bytearray(b'\x00\x02\x03*')
```

---

[13]cf. Python Docs: "bytearray"

```
# Bytearrays can only hold "bytes"
# (integers in the range 0 <= x <= 255)
>>> arr[1] = 'hello'
TypeError: "an integer is required"

>>> arr[1] = 300
ValueError: "byte must be in range(0, 256)"

# Bytearrays can be converted back into bytes objects:
# (This will copy the data)
>>> bytes(arr)
b'\x00\x02\x03*'
```

Key Takeaways

There are a number of built-in data structures you can choose from when it comes to implementing arrays in Python. In this chapter we've focused on core language features and data structures included in the standard library only.

If you're willing to go beyond the Python standard library, third-party packages like *NumPy*[14] offer a wide range of fast array implementations for scientific computing and data science.

By restricting ourselves to the array data structures included with Python, here's what our choices come down to:

You need to store arbitrary objects, potentially with mixed data types? Use a `list` or a `tuple`, depending on whether you want an immutable data structure or not.

You have numeric (integer or floating point) data and tight packing and performance is important? Try out `array.array` and see if it does everything you need. Also, consider going beyond the standard library and try out packages like *NumPy* or *Pandas*.

---

[14]www.numpy.org

You have textual data represented as Unicode characters?
Use Python's built-in `str`. If you need a "mutable string," use a `list`
of characters.

You want to store a contiguous block of bytes? Use the immutable `bytes` type, or `bytearray` if you need a mutable data structure.

In most cases, I like to start out with a simple `list`. I'll only specialize
later on if performance or storage space becomes an issue. Most of
the time, using a general-purpose array data structure like `list` gives
you the fastest development speed and the most programming convenience.

I found that this is usually much more important in the beginning
than trying to squeeze out every last drop of performance right from
the start.

5.3   Records, Structs, and Data Transfer Objects

Compared to arrays, record data structures provide a fixed number of fields, where each field can have a name and may also have a different type.

In this chapter, you'll see how to implement records, structs, and "plain old data objects" in Python, using only built-in data types and classes from the standard library.

By the way, I'm using the definition of a *record* loosely here. For example, I'm also going to discuss types like Python's built-in tuple that may or may not be considered records in a strict sense because they don't provide named fields.

Python offers several data types you can use to implement records, structs, and data transfer objects. In this chapter, you'll get a quick look at each implementation and its unique characteristics. At the end, you'll find a summary and a decision-making guide that will help you make your own picks.

Alright, let's get started!

dict – Simple Data Objects

Python dictionaries store an arbitrary number of objects, each identified by a unique key.[15] Dictionaries are also often called *maps* or *associative arrays* and allow for the efficient lookup, insertion, and deletion of any object associated with a given key.

Using dictionaries as a record data type or data object in Python is possible. Dictionaries are easy to create in Python, as they have their own syntactic sugar built into the language in the form of dictionary literals. The dictionary syntax is concise and quite convenient to type.

---

[15]cf. "Dictionaries, Maps, and Hashtables" chapter

Data objects created using dictionaries are mutable, and there's little protection against misspelled field names, as fields can be added and removed freely at any time. Both of these properties can introduce surprising bugs, and there's always a trade-off to be made between convenience and error resilience.

```python
car1 = {
    'color': 'red',
    'mileage': 3812.4,
    'automatic': True,
}
car2 = {
    'color': 'blue',
    'mileage': 40231,
    'automatic': False,
}

# Dicts have a nice repr:
>>> car2
{'color': 'blue', 'automatic': False, 'mileage': 40231}

# Get mileage:
>>> car2['mileage']
40231

# Dicts are mutable:
>>> car2['mileage'] = 12
>>> car2['windshield'] = 'broken'
>>> car2
{'windshield': 'broken', 'color': 'blue',
 'automatic': False, 'mileage': 12}

# No protection against wrong field names,
# or missing/extra fields:
car3 = {
    'colr': 'green',
```

```
    'automatic': False,
    'windshield': 'broken',
}
```

tuple – Immutable Groups of Objects

Python's tuples are simple data structures for grouping arbitrary objects.[16] Tuples are immutable—they cannot be modified once they've been created.

Performance-wise, tuples take up slightly less memory than lists in CPython,[17] and they're also faster to construct.

As you can see in the bytecode disassembly below, constructing a tuple constant takes a single LOAD_CONST opcode, while constructing a list object with the same contents requires several more operations:

```
>>> import dis
>>> dis.dis(compile("(23, 'a', 'b', 'c')", '', 'eval'))
          0 LOAD_CONST               4 ((23, 'a', 'b', 'c'))
          3 RETURN_VALUE

>>> dis.dis(compile("[23, 'a', 'b', 'c']", '', 'eval'))
          0 LOAD_CONST               0 (23)
          3 LOAD_CONST               1 ('a')
          6 LOAD_CONST               2 ('b')
          9 LOAD_CONST               3 ('c')
         12 BUILD_LIST               4
         15 RETURN_VALUE
```

However, you shouldn't place too much emphasis on these differences. In practice, the performance difference will often be negligible, and trying to squeeze extra performance out of a program by switching from lists to tuples will likely be the wrong approach.

---

[16]cf. Python Docs: "tuple"
[17]cf. CPython tupleobject.c and listobject.c

A potential downside of plain tuples is that the data you store in them can only be pulled out by accessing it through integer indexes. You can't give names to individual properties stored in a tuple. This can impact code readability.

Also, a tuple is always an ad-hoc structure: It's difficult to ensure that two tuples have the same number of fields and the same properties stored on them.

This makes it easy to introduce "slip-of-the-mind" bugs, such as mixing up the field order. Therefore, I would recommend that you keep the number of fields stored in a tuple as low as possible.

```python
# Fields: color, mileage, automatic
>>> car1 = ('red', 3812.4, True)
>>> car2 = ('blue', 40231.0, False)

# Tuple instances have a nice repr:
>>> car1
('red', 3812.4, True)
>>> car2
('blue', 40231.0, False)

# Get mileage:
>>> car2[1]
40231.0

# Tuples are immutable:
>>> car2[1] = 12
TypeError:
"'tuple' object does not support item assignment"

# No protection against missing/extra fields
# or a wrong order:
>>> car3 = (3431.5, 'green', True, 'silver')
```

Writing a Custom Class – More Work, More Control

Classes allow you to define reusable "blueprints" for data objects to ensure each object provides the same set of fields.

Using regular Python classes as record data types is feasible, but it also takes manual work to get the convenience features of other implementations. For example, adding new fields to the __init__ constructor is verbose and takes time.

Also, the default string representation for objects instantiated from custom classes is not very helpful. To fix that you may have to add your own __repr__ method,[18] which again is usually quite verbose and must be updated every time you add a new field.

Fields stored on classes are mutable, and new fields can be added freely, which you may or may not like. It's possible to provide more access control and to create read-only fields using the @property decorator,[19] but once again, this requires writing more glue code.

Writing a custom class is a great option whenever you'd like to add business logic and *behavior* to your record objects using methods. However, this means that these objects are technically no longer plain data objects.

```
class Car:
    def __init__(self, color, mileage, automatic):
        self.color = color
        self.mileage = mileage
        self.automatic = automatic

>>> car1 = Car('red', 3812.4, True)
>>> car2 = Car('blue', 40231.0, False)
```

---

[18] cf. "String Conversion (Every Class Needs a __repr__)" chapter
[19] cf. Python Docs: "property"

179

```
# Get the mileage:
>>> car2.mileage
40231.0

# Classes are mutable:
>>> car2.mileage = 12
>>> car2.windshield = 'broken'

# String representation is not very useful
# (must add a manually written __repr__ method):
>>> car1
<Car object at 0x1081e69e8>
```

collections.namedtuple – Convenient Data Objects

The namedtuple class available in Python 2.6+ provides an extension of the built-in tuple data type.[20] Similar to defining a custom class, using namedtuple allows you to define reusable "blueprints" for your records that ensure the correct field names are used.

Namedtuples are immutable, just like regular tuples. This means you cannot add new fields or modify existing fields after the namedtuple instance was created.

Besides that, namedtuples are, well... named tuples. Each object stored in them can be accessed through a unique identifier. This frees you from having to remember integer indexes, or resort to workarounds like defining integer constants as mnemonics for your indexes.

Namedtuple objects are implemented as regular Python classes internally. When it comes to memory usage, they are also "better" than regular classes and just as memory efficient as regular tuples:

---

[20]cf. "What Namedtuples Are Good For" chapter

```
>>> from collections import namedtuple
>>> from sys import getsizeof

>>> p1 = namedtuple('Point', 'x y z')(1, 2, 3)
>>> p2 = (1, 2, 3)

>>> getsizeof(p1)
72
>>> getsizeof(p2)
72
```

Namedtuples can be an easy way to clean up your code and make it more readable by enforcing a better structure for your data.

I find that going from ad-hoc data types, like dictionaries with a fixed format, to namedtuples helps me express the intent of my code more clearly. Often when I apply this refactoring, I magically come up with a better solution for the problem I'm facing.

Using namedtuples over regular (unstructured) tuples and dicts can also make my coworkers' lives easier: Namedtuples make the data that's being passed around "self-documenting", at least to a degree.

```
>>> from collections import namedtuple
>>> Car = namedtuple('Car' , 'color mileage automatic')
>>> car1 = Car('red', 3812.4, True)

# Instances have a nice repr:
>>> car1
Car(color='red', mileage=3812.4, automatic=True)

# Accessing fields:
>>> car1.mileage
3812.4

# Fields are immtuable:
```

```
>>> car1.mileage = 12
AttributeError: "can't set attribute"
>>> car1.windshield = 'broken'
AttributeError:
"'Car' object has no attribute 'windshield'"
```

typing.NamedTuple – Improved Namedtuples

This class added in Python 3.6 is the younger sibling of the namedtuple class in the collections module.[21] It is very similar to namedtuple, the main difference being an updated syntax for defining new record types and added support for type hints.

Please note that type annotations are not enforced without a separate type-checking tool like *mypy*.[22] But even without tool support, they can provide useful hints for other programmers (or be terribly confusing if the type hints become out-of-date.)

```
>>> from typing import NamedTuple

class Car(NamedTuple):
    color: str
    mileage: float
    automatic: bool

>>> car1 = Car('red', 3812.4, True)

# Instances have a nice repr:
>>> car1
Car(color='red', mileage=3812.4, automatic=True)

# Accessing fields:
>>> car1.mileage
3812.4
```

---

[21]cf. Python Docs: "typing.NamedTuple"

[22]mypy-lang.org

```
# Fields are immutable:
>>> car1.mileage = 12
AttributeError: "can't set attribute"
>>> car1.windshield = 'broken'
AttributeError:
"'Car' object has no attribute 'windshield'"

# Type annotations are not enforced without
# a separate type checking tool like mypy:
>>> Car('red', 'NOT_A_FLOAT', 99)
Car(color='red', mileage='NOT_A_FLOAT', automatic=99)
```

struct.Struct – Serialized C Structs

The struct.Struct class[23] converts between Python values and C structs serialized into Python bytes objects. For example, it can be used to handle binary data stored in files or coming in from network connections.

Structs are defined using a format strings-like mini language that allows you to define the arrangement of various C data types like char, int, and long, as well as their unsigned variants.

Serialized structs are seldom used to represent data objects meant to be handled purely inside Python code. They're intended primarily as a data exchange format, rather than as a way of holding data in memory that's only used by Python code.

In some cases, packing primitive data into structs may use less memory than keeping it in other data types. However, in most cases that would be quite an advanced (and probably unnecessary) optimization.

```
>>> from struct import Struct
>>> MyStruct = Struct('i?f')
>>> data = MyStruct.pack(23, False, 42.0)
```

---

[23]cf. Python Docs: "struct.Struct"

```
# All you get is a blob of data:
>>> data
b'\x17\x00\x00\x00\x00\x00\x00\x00\x00\x00(B'

# Data blobs can be unpacked again:
>>> MyStruct.unpack(data)
(23, False, 42.0)
```

types.SimpleNamespace – Fancy Attribute Access

Here's one more "esoteric" choice for implementing data objects in Python: types.SimpleNamespace.[24] This class was added in Python 3.3 and it provides attribute access to its namespace.

This means SimpleNamespace instances expose all of their keys as class attributes. This means you can use obj.key "dotted" attribute access instead of the obj['key'] square-brackets indexing syntax that's used by regular dicts. All instances also include a meaningful __repr__ by default.

As its name proclaims, SimpleNamespace is simple! It's basically a glorified dictionary that allows attribute access and prints nicely. Attributes can be added, modified, and deleted freely.

```
>>> from types import SimpleNamespace
>>> car1 = SimpleNamespace(color='red',
...                        mileage=3812.4,
...                        automatic=True)

# The default repr:
>>> car1
namespace(automatic=True, color='red', mileage=3812.4)

# Instances support attribute access and are mutable:
```

---

[24]cf. Python Docs: "types.SimpleNamespace"

```
>>> car1.mileage = 12
>>> car1.windshield = 'broken'
>>> del car1.automatic
>>> car1
namespace(color='red', mileage=12, windshield='broken')
```

Key Takeaways

Now, which type should you use for data objects in Python? As you've seen, there's quite a number of different options for implementing records or data objects. Generally your decision will depend on your use case:

You only have a few (2-3) fields: Using a plain tuple object may be okay if the field order is easy to remember or field names are superfluous. For example, think of an (x, y, z) point in 3D space.

You need immutable fields: In this case, plain tuples, collections.namedtuple, and typing.NamedTuple would all make good options for implementing this type of data object.

You need to lock down field names to avoid typos: collections.namedtuple and typing.NamedTuple are your friends here.

You want to keep things simple: A plain dictionary object might be a good choice due to the convenient syntax that closely resembles JSON.

You need full control over your data structure: It's time to write a custom class with @property setters and getters.

You need to add behavior (methods) to the object: You should write a custom class, either from scratch or by extending collections.namedtuple or typing.NamedTuple.

You need to pack data tightly to serialize it to disk or to send it over the network: Time to read up on struct.Struct because

185

this is a great use case for it.

If you're looking for a safe default choice, my general recommendation for implementing a plain record, struct, or data object in Python would be to use `collections.namedtuple` in Python 2.x and its younger sibling, `typing.NamedTuple` in Python 3.

5.4 Sets and Multisets

In this chapter you'll see how to implement mutable and immutable set and multiset (bag) data structures in Python, using built-in data types and classes from the standard library. First though, let's do a quick recap of what a set data structure is:

A *set* is an unordered collection of objects that does not allow duplicate elements. Typically, sets are used to quickly test a value for membership in the set, to insert or delete new values from a set, and to compute the union or intersection of two sets.

In a "proper" set implementation, membership tests are expected to run in fast *O(1)* time. Union, intersection, difference, and subset operations should take *O(n)* time on average. The set implementations included in Python's standard library follow these performance characteristics.[25]

Just like dictionaries, sets get special treatment in Python and have some syntactic sugar that makes them easy to create. For example, the curly-braces set expression syntax and set comprehensions allow you to conveniently define new set instances:

```python
vowels = {'a', 'e', 'i', 'o', 'u'}
squares = {x * x for x in range(10)}
```

But be careful: To create *an empty set* you'll need to call the set() constructor. Using empty curly-braces {} is ambiguous and will create an empty dictionary instead.

Python and its standard library provide several set implementations. Let's have a look at them.

---

[25]cf. wiki.python.org/moin/TimeComplexity

set – Your Go-To Set

This is the built-in set implementation in Python.[26] The set type is mutable and allows for the dynamic insertion and deletion of elements.

Python's sets are backed by the dict data type and share the same performance characteristics. Any hashable object can be stored in a set.[27]

```
>>> vowels = {'a', 'e', 'i', 'o', 'u'}
>>> 'e' in vowels
True

>>> letters = set('alice')
>>> letters.intersection(vowels)
{'a', 'e', 'i'}

>>> vowels.add('x')
>>> vowels
{'i', 'a', 'u', 'o', 'x', 'e'}

>>> len(vowels)
6
```

frozenset – Immutable Sets

The frozenset class implements an *immutable* version of set that cannot be changed after it has been constructed.[28] Frozensets are static and only allow query operations on their elements (no inserts or deletions.) Because frozensets are static and hashable, they can be used as dictionary keys or as elements of another set, something that isn't possible with regular (mutable) set objects.

---

[26]cf. Python Docs: "set"
[27]cf. Python Docs: "hashable"
[28]cf. Python Docs: "frozenset"

```
>>> vowels = frozenset({'a', 'e', 'i', 'o', 'u'})
>>> vowels.add('p')
AttributeError:
"'frozenset' object has no attribute 'add'"

# Frozensets are hashable and can
# be used as dictionary keys:
>>> d = { frozenset({1, 2, 3}): 'hello' }
>>> d[frozenset({1, 2, 3})]
'hello'
```

collections.Counter – Multisets

The collections.Counter class in the Python standard library implements a multiset (or bag) type that allows elements in the set to have more than one occurrence.[29]

This is useful if you need to keep track of not only *if* an element is part of a set, but also *how many times* it is included in the set:

```
>>> from collections import Counter
>>> inventory = Counter()

>>> loot = {'sword': 1, 'bread': 3}
>>> inventory.update(loot)
>>> inventory
Counter({'bread': 3, 'sword': 1})

>>> more_loot = {'sword': 1, 'apple': 1}
>>> inventory.update(more_loot)
>>> inventory
Counter({'bread': 3, 'sword': 2, 'apple': 1})
```

Here's a caveat for the Counter class: You'll want to be careful when counting the number of elements in a Counter object. Calling len()

---

[29]cf. Python Docs: "collections.Counter"

returns the number of *unique* elements in the multiset, whereas the total number of elements can be retrieved using the sum function:

```
>>> len(inventory)
3  # Unique elements

>>> sum(inventory.values())
6  # Total no. of elements
```

Key Takeaways

- Sets are another useful and commonly used data structure included with Python and its standard library.
- Use the built-in `set` type when looking for a mutable set.
- `frozenset` objects are hashable and can be used as dictionary or set keys.
- `collections.Counter` implements multiset or "bag" data structures.

5.5 Stacks (LIFOs)

A stack is a collection of objects that supports fast *last-in, first-out (LIFO)* semantics for inserts and deletes. Unlike lists or arrays, stacks typically don't allow for random access to the objects they contain. The insert and delete operations are also often called *push* and *pop*.

A useful real-world analogy for a stack data structure is a *stack of plates*:

> *New plates are added to the top of the stack. And because the plates are precious and heavy, only the topmost plate can be moved (last-in, first-out). To reach the plates that are lower down in the stack, the topmost plates must be removed one by one.*

Stacks and queues are similar. They're both linear collections of items, and the difference lies in the order that the items are accessed:

With a **queue**, you remove the item *least* recently added (*first-in, first-out* or *FIFO*); but with a **stack**, you remove the item *most* recently added (*last-in, first-out* or *LIFO*).

Performance-wise, a proper stack implementation is expected to take $O(1)$ time for insert and delete operations.

Stacks have a wide range of uses in algorithms, for example, in language parsing and runtime memory management ("call stack"). A short and beautiful algorithm using a stack is depth-first search (DFS) on a tree or graph data structure.

Python ships with several stack implementations that each have slightly different characteristics. We'll now take a look at them and compare their characteristics.

`list` – Simple, Built-In Stacks

Python's built-in `list` type makes a decent stack data structure as it supports push and pop operations in amortized $O(1)$ time.[30]

Python's lists are implemented as dynamic arrays internally, which means they occasionally need to resize the storage space for elements stored in them when elements are added or removed. The list over-allocates its backing storage so that not every push or pop requires resizing, and as a result, you get an amortized $O(1)$ time complexity for these operations.

The downside is that this makes their performance less consistent than the stable $O(1)$ inserts and deletes provided by a linked list based implementation (like `collections.deque`, see below). On the other hand, lists do provide fast $O(1)$ time random access to elements on the stack, and this can be an added benefit.

Here's an important performance caveat you should be aware of when using lists as stacks:

To get the amortized $O(1)$ performance for inserts and deletes, new items must be added to the *end* of the list with the append() method and removed again from the end using pop(). For optimum performance, stacks based on Python lists should grow towards higher indexes and shrink towards lower ones.

Adding and removing from the front is much slower and takes $O(n)$ time, as the existing elements must be shifted around to make room for the new element. This is a performance antipattern that you should avoid as much as possible.

```
>>> s = []
>>> s.append('eat')
>>> s.append('sleep')
>>> s.append('code')
```

---

[30] cf. Python Docs: "Using lists as stacks"

```
>>> s
['eat', 'sleep', 'code']

>>> s.pop()
'code'
>>> s.pop()
'sleep'
>>> s.pop()
'eat'

>>> s.pop()
IndexError: "pop from empty list"
```

collections.deque – Fast & Robust Stacks

The deque class implements a double-ended queue that supports adding and removing elements from either end in $O(1)$ time (non-amortized). Because deques support adding and removing elements from either end equally well, they can serve both as queues and as stacks.[31]

Python's deque objects are implemented as doubly-linked lists which gives them excellent and consistent performance for inserting and deleting elements, but poor $O(n)$ performance for randomly accessing elements in the middle of a stack.[32]

Overall, collections.deque is a great choice if you're looking for a stack data structure in Python's standard library that has the performance characteristics of a linked-list implementation.

```
>>> from collections import deque
>>> s = deque()
>>> s.append('eat')
>>> s.append('sleep')
```

---

[31]cf. Python Docs: "collections.deque"
[32]cf. CPython _collectionsmodule.c

```
>>> s.append('code')

>>> s
deque(['eat', 'sleep', 'code'])

>>> s.pop()
'code'
>>> s.pop()
'sleep'
>>> s.pop()
'eat'

>>> s.pop()
IndexError: "pop from an empty deque"
```

queue.LifoQueue – Locking Semantics for Parallel Computing

This stack implementation in the Python standard library is synchronized and provides locking semantics to support multiple concurrent producers and consumers.[33]

Besides LifoQueue, the queue module contains several other classes that implement multi-producer/multi-consumer queues that are useful for parallel computing.

Depending on your use case, the locking semantics might be helpful, or they might just incur unneeded overhead. In this case you'd be better off with using a list or a deque as a general-purpose stack.

```
>>> from queue import LifoQueue
>>> s = LifoQueue()
>>> s.put('eat')
>>> s.put('sleep')
>>> s.put('code')
```

---

[33]cf. Python Docs: "queue.LifoQueue"

```
>>> s
<queue.LifoQueue object at 0x108298dd8>

>>> s.get()
'code'
>>> s.get()
'sleep'
>>> s.get()
'eat'

>>> s.get_nowait()
queue.Empty

>>> s.get()
# Blocks / waits forever...
```

Comparing Stack Implementations in Python

As you've seen, Python ships with several implementations for a stack data structure. All of them have slightly different characteristics, as well as performance and usage trade-offs.

If you're not looking for parallel processing support (or don't want to handle locking and unlocking manually), your choice comes down to the built-in list type or collections.deque. The difference lies in the data structure used behind the scenes and overall ease of use:

- list is backed by a dynamic array which makes it great for fast random access, but requires occasional resizing when elements are added or removed. The list over-allocates its backing storage so that not every push or pop requires resizing, and you get an amortized *O(1)* time complexity for these operations. But you do need to be careful to only insert and remove items "from the right side" using append() and pop(). Otherwise, performance slows down to *O(n)*.

- `collections.deque` is backed by a doubly-linked list which optimizes appends and deletes at both ends and provides consistent *O(1)* performance for these operations. Not only is its performance more stable, the deque class is also easier to use because you don't have to worry about adding or removing items from "the wrong end."

In summary, I believe that `collections.deque` is an excellent choice for implementing a stack (LIFO queue) in Python.

Key Takeaways

- Python ships with several stack implementations that have slightly different performance and usage characteristics.
- `collections.deque` provides a safe and fast general-purpose stack implementation.
- The built-in `list` type can be used as a stack, but be careful to only append and remove items with `append()` and `pop()` in order to avoid slow performance.

5.6 Queues (FIFOs)

In this chapter you'll see how to implement a FIFO queue data structure using only built-in data types and classes from the Python standard library. But first, let's recap what a queue is:

A queue is a collection of objects that supports fast *first-in, first-out (FIFO)* semantics for inserts and deletes. The insert and delete operations are sometimes called *enqueue* and *dequeue*. Unlike lists or arrays, queues typically don't allow for random access to the objects they contain.

Here's a real-world analogy for a first-in, first-out queue:

> *Imagine a line of Pythonistas waiting to pick up their conference badges on day one of PyCon registration. New additions to the line are made to the back of the queue as new people enter the conference venue and "queue up" to receive their badges. Removal (serving) happens in the front of the queue, as developers receive their badges and conference swag bags and leave the queue.*

Another way to memorize the characteristics of a queue data structure is to think of it as a *pipe*:

> *New items (water molecules, ping-pong balls, ...) are put in at one end and travel to the other where you or someone else removes them again. While the items are in the queue (a solid metal pipe) you can't get at them. The only way to interact with the items in the queue is to add new items at the back (*enqueue*) or to remove items at the front (*dequeue*) of the pipe.*

Queues are similar to stacks, and the difference between them lies in how items are removed:

With a **queue**, you remove the item *least* recently added (*first-in, first-out* or *FIFO*); but with a **stack**, you remove the item *most* recently added (*last-in, first-out* or *LIFO*).

Performance-wise, a proper queue implementation is expected to take *O(1)* time for insert and delete operations. These are the two main operations performed on a queue, and in a correct implementation, they should be fast.

Queues have a wide range of applications in algorithms and often help solve scheduling and parallel programming problems. A short and beautiful algorithm using a queue is breadth-first search (BFS) on a tree or graph data structure.

Scheduling algorithms often use priority queues internally. These are specialized queues: Instead of retrieving the next element by insertion time, a priority queue retrieves the *highest-priority* element. The priority of individual elements is decided by the queue, based on the ordering applied to their keys. We'll take a closer look at priority queues and how they're implemented in Python in the next chapter.

A regular queue, however, won't re-order the items it carries. Just like in the pipe example, "you'll get what you put in" and in exactly that order.

Python ships with several queue implementations that each have slightly different characteristics. Let's review them.

`list` — Terribly Sloooow Queues

It's possible to use a regular `list` as a queue but this is not ideal from a performance perspective.[34] Lists are quite slow for this purpose because inserting or deleting an element at the beginning requires shifting all of the other elements by one, requiring *O(n)* time.

Therefore, I would *not recommend* using a `list` as a makeshift queue in Python (unless you're only dealing with a small number of

---

[34]cf. Python Docs: "Using lists as queues"

elements).

```
>>> q = []
>>> q.append('eat')
>>> q.append('sleep')
>>> q.append('code')

>>> q
['eat', 'sleep', 'code']

# Careful: This is slow!
>>> q.pop(0)
'eat'
```

collections.deque – Fast & Robust Queues

The deque class implements a double-ended queue that supports adding and removing elements from either end in $O(1)$ time (non-amortized). Because deques support adding and removing elements from either end equally well, they can serve both as queues and as stacks.[35]

Python's deque objects are implemented as doubly-linked lists.[36] This gives them excellent and consistent performance for inserting and deleting elements, but poor $O(n)$ performance for randomly accessing elements in the middle of the stack.

As a result, collections.deque is a great default choice if you're looking for a queue data structure in Python's standard library.

```
>>> from collections import deque
>>> q = deque()
>>> q.append('eat')
>>> q.append('sleep')
```

---

[35]cf. Python Docs: "collections.deque"
[36]cf. CPython _collectionsmodule.c

```
>>> q.append('code')

>>> q
deque(['eat', 'sleep', 'code'])

>>> q.popleft()
'eat'
>>> q.popleft()
'sleep'
>>> q.popleft()
'code'

>>> q.popleft()
IndexError: "pop from an empty deque"
```

queue.Queue – Locking Semantics for Parallel Computing

This queue implementation in the Python standard library is synchronized and provides locking semantics to support multiple concurrent producers and consumers.[37]

The queue module contains several other classes implementing multi-producer/multi-consumer queues that are useful for parallel computing.

Depending on your use case, the locking semantics might be helpful or just incur unneeded overhead. In this case, you'd be better off using collections.deque as a general-purpose queue.

```
>>> from queue import Queue
>>> q = Queue()
>>> q.put('eat')
>>> q.put('sleep')
>>> q.put('code')
```

---

[37]cf. Python Docs: "queue.Queue"

```
>>> q
<queue.Queue object at 0x1070f5b38>

>>> q.get()
'eat'
>>> q.get()
'sleep'
>>> q.get()
'code'

>>> q.get_nowait()
queue.Empty

>>> q.get()
# Blocks / waits forever...
```

multiprocessing.Queue – Shared Job Queues

This is a shared job queue implementation that allows queued items to be processed in parallel by multiple concurrent workers.[38] Process-based parallelization is popular in CPython due to the global interpreter lock (GIL) that prevents some forms of parallel execution on a single interpreter process.

As a specialized queue implementation meant for sharing data between processes, multiprocessing.Queue makes it easy to distribute work across multiple processes in order to work around the GIL limitations. This type of queue can store and transfer any pickle-able object across process boundaries.

```
>>> from multiprocessing import Queue
>>> q = Queue()
>>> q.put('eat')
>>> q.put('sleep')
```

---

[38]cf. Python Docs: "multiprocessing.Queue"

```
>>> q.put('code')

>>> q
<multiprocessing.queues.Queue object at 0x1081c12b0>

>>> q.get()
'eat'
>>> q.get()
'sleep'
>>> q.get()
'code'

>>> q.get()
# Blocks / waits forever...
```

Key Takeaways

- Python includes several queue implementations as part of the core language and its standard library.
- `list` objects can be used as queues, but this is generally not recommended due to slow performance.
- If you're not looking for parallel processing support, the implementation offered by `collections.deque` is an excellent default choice for implementing a FIFO queue data structure in Python. It provides the performance characteristics you'd expect from a good queue implementation and can also be used as a stack (LIFO Queue).

5.7 Priority Queues

A priority queue is a container data structure that manages a set of records with totally-ordered[39] keys (for example, a numeric *weight* value) to provide quick access to the record with the *smallest* or *largest* key in the set.

You can think of a priority queue as a modified queue: instead of re-trieving the next element by insertion time, it retrieves the *highest-priority* element. The priority of individual elements is decided by the ordering applied to their keys.

Priority queues are commonly used for dealing with scheduling prob-lems, for example, to give precedence to tasks with higher urgency.

Think about the job of an operating system task scheduler:

> *Ideally, high-priority tasks on the system (e.g., play-ing a real-time game) should take precedence over lower-priority tasks (e.g., downloading updates in the background). By organizing pending tasks in a priority queue that uses the task urgency as the key, the task scheduler can quickly select the highest-priority tasks and allow them to run first.*

In this chapter you'll see a few options for how you can implement Priority Queues in Python using built-in data structures or data struc-tures that ship with Python's standard library. Each implementation will have their own upsides and downsides, but in my mind there's a clear winner for most common scenarios. Let's find out which one it is.

`list` – Maintaining a Manually Sorted Queue

You can use a sorted `list` to quickly identify and delete the smallest or largest element. The downside is that inserting new elements into

---

[39]cf. Wikipedia "Total order"

a list is a slow *O(n)* operation.

While the insertion point can be found in *O(log n)* time using `bisect.insort`[40] in the standard library, this is always dominated by the slow insertion step.

Maintaining the order by appending to the list and re-sorting also takes at least *O(n log n)* time. Another downside is that you must manually take care of re-sorting the list when new elements are inserted. It's easy to introduce bugs by missing this step, and the burden is always on you, the developer.

Therefore, I believe that sorted lists are only suitable as priority queues when there will be few insertions.

```python
q = []

q.append((2, 'code'))
q.append((1, 'eat'))
q.append((3, 'sleep'))

# NOTE: Remember to re-sort every time
#       a new element is inserted, or use
#       bisect.insort().
q.sort(reverse=True)

while q:
    next_item = q.pop()
    print(next_item)

# Result:
#    (1, 'eat')
#    (2, 'code')
#    (3, 'sleep')
```

---

[40]cf. Python Docs: "bisect.insort"

heapq – List-Based Binary Heaps

This is a binary heap implementation usually backed by a plain list, and it supports insertion and extraction of the smallest element in $O(log\ n)$ time.[41]

This module is a good choice for implementing priority queues in Python. Since heapq technically only provides a min-heap implementation, extra steps must be taken to ensure sort stability and other features typically expected from a "practical" priority queue.[42]

```
import heapq

q = []

heapq.heappush(q, (2, 'code'))
heapq.heappush(q, (1, 'eat'))
heapq.heappush(q, (3, 'sleep'))

while q:
    next_item = heapq.heappop(q)
    print(next_item)

# Result:
#    (1, 'eat')
#    (2, 'code')
#    (3, 'sleep')
```

queue.PriorityQueue – Beautiful Priority Queues

This priority queue implementation uses heapq internally and shares the same time and space complexities.[43]

---

[41]cf. Python Docs: "heapq"
[42]cf. Python Docs: "heapq – Priority queue implementation notes"
[43]cf. Python Docs: "queue.PriorityQueue"

The difference is that PriorityQueue is synchronized and provides locking semantics to support multiple concurrent producers and consumers.

Depending on your use case, this might be helpful—or just slow your program down slightly. In any case, you might prefer the class-based interface provided by PriorityQueue over using the function-based interface provided by heapq.

```python
from queue import PriorityQueue

q = PriorityQueue()

q.put((2, 'code'))
q.put((1, 'eat'))
q.put((3, 'sleep'))

while not q.empty():
    next_item = q.get()
    print(next_item)

# Result:
#     (1, 'eat')
#     (2, 'code')
#     (3, 'sleep')
```

Key Takeaways

- Python includes several priority queue implementations for you to use.
- queue.PriorityQueue stands out from the pack with a nice object-oriented interface and a name that clearly states its intent. It should be your preferred choice.
- If you'd like to avoid the locking overhead of queue.PriorityQueue, using the heapq module directly is also a good option.

Chapter 6

Looping & Iteration

6.1 Writing Pythonic Loops

One of the easiest ways to spot a developer with a background in C-style languages who only recently picked up Python is to look at how they write loops.

For example, whenever I see a code snippet like the following, that's an example of someone trying to write Python like it's C or Java:

```python
my_items = ['a', 'b', 'c']

i = 0
while i < len(my_items):
    print(my_items[i])
    i += 1
```

Now, what's so "unpythonic" about this code, you ask? Two things:

First, it keeps track of the index i manually—initializing, it to zero and then carefully incrementing it upon every loop iteration.

And second, it uses len() to get the size of the my_items container in order to determine how often to iterate.

In Python you can write loops that handle both of these responsibilities automatically. It's a great idea to take advantage of that. For example, it's much harder to write accidental infinite loops if your code doesn't have to keep track of a running index. It also makes the code more concise and therefore more readable.

To refactor this first code example, I'll start by removing the code that manually updates the index. A good way to do that is with a for-loop in Python. Using the range() built-in, I can generate the indexes automatically:

```python
>>> range(len(my_items))
range(0, 3)
```

```
>>> list(range(0, 3))
[0, 1, 2]
```

The range type represents an immutable sequence of numbers. Its advantage over a regular list is that it always takes the same small amount of memory. Range objects don't actually store the individual values representing the number sequence—instead, they function as iterators and calculate the sequence values on the fly.[1]

So, rather than incrementing i manually on each loop iteration, I could take advantage of the range() function and write something like this:

```
for i in range(len(my_items)):
    print(my_items[i])
```

This is better. However, it still isn't very Pythonic and it still feels more like a Java-esque iteration construct than a proper Python loop. When you see code that uses range(len(...)) to iterate over a container you can usually simplify and improve it further.

As I mentioned, in Python, for-loops are really "for-each" loops that can iterate directly over items from a container or sequence, without having to look them up by index. I can use this to simplify this loop even more:

```
for item in my_items:
    print(item)
```

I would consider this solution to be quite Pythonic. It uses several advanced Python features but remains nice and clean and almost reads like pseudo code from a programming textbook. Notice how this loop

---

[1]In Python 2 you'll need to use the xrange() built-in to get this memory-saving behavior, as range() will actually construct a list object.

no longer keeps track of the container's size and doesn't use a running index to access elements.

The container itself now takes care of handing out the elements so they can be processed. If the container is ordered, the resulting sequence of elements will be too. If the container isn't ordered, it will return its elements in arbitrary order but the loop will still cover all of them.

Now, of course you won't always be able to rewrite your loops like that. What if you *need* the item index, for example?

It's possible to write loops that keep a running index while avoiding the range(len(...)) pattern I cautioned against. The enumerate() built-in helps you make those kinds of loops nice and Pythonic:

```
>>> for i, item in enumerate(my_items):
...         print(f'{i}: {item}')

0: a
1: b
2: c
```

You see, iterators in Python can return more than just one value. They can return tuples with an arbitrary number of values that can then be unpacked right inside the for-statement.

This is very powerful. For example, you can use the same technique to iterate over the keys and values of a dictionary at the same time:

```
>>> emails = {
...         'Bob': 'bob@example.com',
...         'Alice': 'alice@example.com',
... }

>>> for name, email in emails.items():
...         print(f'{name} -> {email}')
```

```
'Bob -> bob@example.com'
'Alice -> alice@example.com'
```

There's one more example I'd like to show you. What if you absolutely, positively need to write a C-style loop. For example, what if you must control the step size for the index? Imagine you started out with the following Java loop:

```
for (int i = a; i < n; i += s) {
    // ...
}
```

How would this pattern translate to Python? The range() function comes to our rescue again—it accepts optional parameters to control the start value for the loop (a), the stop value (n), and the step size (s). Therefore, our Java loop example could be translated to Python, like this:

```
for i in range(a, n, s):
    # ...
```

Key Takeaways

- Writing C-style loops in Python is considered unpythonic. Avoid managing loop indexes and stop conditions manually if possible.
- Python's for-loops are really "for-each" loops that can iterate directly over items from a container or sequence.

6.2 Comprehending Comprehensions

One of my favorite features in Python are list comprehensions. They can seem a bit arcane at first but when you break them down they are actually a very simple construct.

The key to understanding list comprehensions is that they're just for-loops over a collection but expressed in a more terse and compact syntax.

This is sometimes referred to as *syntactic sugar*—a little shortcut for frequently used functionality that makes our lives as Python coders easier. Take the following list comprehension as an example:

```
>>> squares = [x * x for x in range(10)]
```

It computes a list of all integer square numbers from zero to nine:

```
>>> squares
[0, 1, 4, 9, 16, 25, 36, 49, 64, 81]
```

If you wanted to build the same list using a plain for-loop, you'd probably write something like this:

```
>>> squares = []
>>> for x in range(10):
...     squares.append(x * x)
```

That's a pretty straightforward loop, right? If you go back and compare the list comprehension example with the for-loop version, you'll spot the commonalities and eventually some patterns will emerge. By generalizing some of the common structure here, you'll eventually end up with a template similar to the one below:

```
values = [expression for item in collection]
```

The above list comprehension "template" is equivalent to the following plain for-loop:

```
values = []
for item in collection:
    values.append(expression)
```

Here, we first set up a new `list` instance to receive the output values. Then, we iterate over all items in the container, transforming each of them with an arbitrary expression and then adding the individual results to the output list.

This is a "cookie-cutter pattern" that you can apply to many for-loops in order to transform them into list comprehensions and vice versa. Now, there's one more useful addition we need to make to this template, and that is filtering elements with *conditions*.

List comprehensions can filter values based on some arbitrary condition that decides whether or not the resulting value becomes a part of the output list. Here's an example:

```
>>> even_squares = [x * x for x in range(10)
                    if x % 2 == 0]
```

This list comprehension will compute a list of the squares of all *even* integers from zero to nine. The *modulo* (%) operator used here returns the remainder after division of one number by another. In this example, we use it to test if a number is even. And it has the desired result:

```
>>> even_squares
[0, 4, 16, 36, 64]
```

Similar to the first example, this new list comprehension can be transformed into an equivalent for-loop:

```
even_squares = []
for x in range(10):
    if x % 2 == 0:
        even_squares.append(x * x)
```

Let's try and generalize the above *list comprehension to for-loop* transformation pattern some more. This time we're going to add a filter condition to our template so we get to decide which values end up in the output list. Here's the updated list comprehension template:

```
values = [expression
          for item in collection
          if condition]
```

Again, we can transform this list comprehension into a *for*-loop with the following pattern:

```
values = []
for item in collection:
    if condition:
        values.append(expression)
```

Once more, this was a straightforward transformation—we simply applied the updated cookie-cutter pattern. I hope this dispels some of the "magic" associated with how list comprehensions work. They're a useful tool that all Python programmers should know how to use.

Before you move on, I want to point out that Python not only supports *list* comprehensions but also has similar syntactic sugar for *sets* and *dictionaries*.

Here's what a *set comprehension* looks like:

```
>>> { x * x for x in range(-9, 10) }
set([64, 1, 36, 0, 49, 9, 16, 81, 25, 4])
```

Unlike lists, which retain the order of the elements in them, Python sets are an unordered collection type. So you'll get a more or less "random" order when you add items to a set container.

And this is a *dictionary comprehension*:

```
>>> { x: x * x for x in range(5) }
{0: 0, 1: 1, 2: 4, 3: 9, 4: 16}
```

Both are useful tools in practice. There's one caveat to Python's comprehensions though—as you get more proficient at using them, it becomes easier and easier to write code that's difficult to read. If you're not careful, you might have to deal with monstrous list, set, and dict comprehensions soon. Remember, too much of a good thing is usually a bad thing.

After much chagrin, I'm personally drawing the line at one level of nesting for comprehensions. I found that in most cases it's better (as in "more readable" and "easier to maintain") to use for-loops beyond that point.

Key Takeaways

- Comprehensions are a key feature in Python. Understanding and applying them will make your code much more Pythonic.
- Comprehensions are just fancy syntactic sugar for a simple for-loop pattern. Once you understand the pattern, you'll develop an intuitive understanding for comprehensions.
- There are more than just list comprehensions.

6.3   List Slicing Tricks and the Sushi Operator

Python's list objects have a neat feature called *slicing*. You can view it as an extension of the square-brackets indexing syntax. Slicing is commonly used to access ranges of elements within an ordered collection. For example, you can slice up a large list object into several smaller sublists with it.

Here's an example. Slicing uses the familiar "[ ]" indexing syntax with the following "[start:stop:step]" pattern:

```
>>> lst = [1, 2, 3, 4, 5]
>>> lst
[1, 2, 3, 4, 5]

#    lst[start:end:step]
>>> lst[1:3:1]
[2, 3]
```

Adding the [1:3:1] index returned a slice of the original list ranging from index 1 to index 2, with a step size of one element. To avoid off-by-one errors, it's important to remember that the upper bound is always exclusive. This is why we got [2, 3] as the sublist from the [1:3:1] slice.

If you leave out the step size, it defaults to one:

```
>>> lst[1:3]
[2, 3]
```

You can do other interesting things with the step parameter, also called the *stride*. For example, you can create a sublist that includes every other element of the original:

```
>>> lst[::2]
[1, 3, 5]
```

Wasn't that fun? I like to call ":" the *sushi operator*. It looks like a delicious maki roll cut in half. Besides reminding you of delicious food and accessing ranges of lists, it has a few more lesser-known applications. Let me show you some more fun and useful list-slicing tricks!

You just saw how the slicing step size can be used to select every other element of a list. Well, there's more: If you ask for a [::-1] slice, you'll get a copy of the original list, but in the reverse order:

```
>>> numbers[::-1]
[5, 4, 3, 2, 1]
```

We asked Python to give us the full list (::), but to go over all of the elements from back to front by setting the step size to -1. This is pretty neat, but in most cases I'd still stick with list.reverse() and the built-in reversed() function to reverse a list.

Here's another list-slicing trick: You can use the :-operator to clear all elements from a list without destroying the list object itself.

This is extremely helpful when you need to clear out a list in your program that has other references pointing to it. In this case, you often can't just empty the list by replacing it with a new list object, since that wouldn't update the other references. But here's the sushi operator coming to your rescue:

```
>>> lst = [1, 2, 3, 4, 5]
>>> del lst[:]
>>> lst
[]
```

As you can see, this removes all elements from lst but leaves the list object itself intact. In Python 3 you can also use lst.clear() for the same job, which might be the more readable pattern, depending on the circumstances. However, keep in mind that clear() isn't available in Python 2.

Besides clearing lists, you can also use slicing to replace all elements of a list without creating a new list object. This is a nice shorthand for clearing a list and then repopulating it manually:

```
>>> original_lst = lst
>>> lst[:] = [7, 8, 9]
>>> lst
[7, 8, 9]
>>> original_lst
[7, 8, 9]
>>> original_lst is lst
True
```

The previous code example replaced all elements in lst but did not destroy and recreate the list itself. The old references to the original list object are therefore still valid.

Yet another use case for the sushi operator is creating (shallow) copies of existing lists:

```
>>> copied_lst = lst[:]
>>> copied_lst
[7, 8, 9]
>>> copied_lst is lst
False
```

Creating a *shallow* copy means that only the structure of the elements is copied, not the elements themselves. Both copies of the list share the same instances of the individual elements.

If you need to duplicate everything, including the elements, then you'll need to create a *deep* copy of the list. Python's built-in copy module will come in handy for this.

Key Takeaways

- The : "sushi operator" is not only useful for selecting sublists of elements within a list. It can also be used to clear, reverse, and copy lists.
- But be careful—this functionality borders on the arcane for many Python developers. Using it might make your code less maintainable for everyone else on your team.

6.4 Beautiful Iterators

I love how beautiful and clear Python's syntax is compared to many other programming languages. Let's take the humble *for-in* loop, for example. It speaks to Python's beauty that you can read a Pythonic loop like this, as if it was an English sentence:

```python
numbers = [1, 2, 3]
for n in numbers:
    print(n)
```

But how do Python's elegant loop constructs work behind the scenes? How does the loop fetch individual elements from the object it is looping over? And, how can you support the same programming style in your own Python objects?

You'll find the answers to these questions in Python's *iterator protocol*: Objects that support the __iter__ and __next__ dunder methods automatically work with *for-in* loops.

But let's take things step by step. Just like decorators, iterators and their related techniques can appear quite arcane and complicated on first glance. So, we'll ease into them.

In this chapter you'll see how to write several Python classes that support the iterator protocol. They'll serve as "non-magical" examples and test implementations you can build upon and deepen your understanding with.

We'll focus on the core mechanics of iterators in Python 3 first and leave out any unnecessary complications, so you can see clearly how iterators behave at the fundamental level.

I'll tie each example back to the *for-in* loop question we started out with. And, at the end of this chapter we'll go over some differences that exist between Python 2 and 3 when it comes to iterators.

Ready? Let's jump right in!

Iterating Forever

We'll begin by writing a class that demonstrates the bare-bones iterator protocol. The example I'm using here might look different from the examples you've seen in other iterator tutorials, but bear with me. I think doing it this way gives you a more applicable understanding of how iterators work in Python.

Over the next few paragraphs we're going to implement a class called Repeater that can be iterated over with a *for-in* loop, like so:

```python
repeater = Repeater('Hello')
for item in repeater:
    print(item)
```

Like its name suggests, instances of this Repeater class will repeatedly return a single value when iterated over. So the above example code would forever print the string 'Hello' to the console.

To start with the implementation, we'll first define and flesh out the Repeater class:

```python
class Repeater:
    def __init__(self, value):
        self.value = value

    def __iter__(self):
        return RepeaterIterator(self)
```

On first inspection, Repeater looks like a bog-standard Python class. But notice how it also includes the __iter__ dunder method.

What's the RepeaterIterator object we're creating and returning from __iter__? It's a helper class we also need to define for our *for-in* iteration example to work:

```python
class RepeaterIterator:
    def __init__(self, source):
        self.source = source

    def __next__(self):
        return self.source.value
```

Again, RepeaterIterator looks like a straightforward Python class, but you might want to take note of the following two things:

1. In the __init__ method, we link each RepeaterIterator instance to the Repeater object that created it. That way we can hold onto the "source" object that's being iterated over.

2. In RepeaterIterator.__next__, we reach back into the "source" Repeater instance and return the value associated with it.

In this code example, Repeater and RepeaterIterator are working *together* to support Python's iterator protocol. The two dunder methods we defined, __iter__ and __next__, are the keys to making a Python object iterable.

We'll take a closer look at these two methods and how they work together after some hands-on experimentation with the code we've got so far.

Let's confirm that this two-class setup really made Repeater objects compatible with *for-in* loop iteration. To do that we'll first create an instance of Repeater that would return the string 'Hello' indefinitely:

```python
>>> repeater = Repeater('Hello')
```

And now we're going to try iterating over this repeater object with a *for-in* loop. What's going to happen when you run the following code snippet?

```
>>> for item in repeater:
...     print(item)
```

Right on! You'll see `'Hello'` printed to the screen...a lot. `Repeater` keeps on returning the same string value, and so, this loop will never complete. Our little program is doomed to forever print `'Hello'` to the console:

```
Hello
Hello
Hello
Hello
Hello
...
```

But congratulations—you just wrote a working iterator in Python and used it with a *for-in* loop. The loop may not terminate yet...but so far, so good!

Next up, we'll tease this example apart to understand how the __iter__ and __next__ methods work together to make a Python object iterable.

Pro tip: If you ran the last example inside a Python REPL session or from the terminal, and you want to stop it, hit *Ctrl + C* a few times to break out of the infinite loop.

How do *for-in* loops work in Python?

At this point we've got our `Repeater` class that apparently supports the iterator protocol, and we just ran a *for-in* loop to prove it:

```
repeater = Repeater('Hello')
for item in repeater:
    print(item)
```

Now, what does this for-in loop really do behind the scenes? How does it communicate with the repeater object to fetch new elements from it?

To dispel some of that "magic," we can expand this loop into a slightly longer code snippet that gives the same result:

```
repeater = Repeater('Hello')
iterator = repeater.__iter__()
while True:
    item = iterator.__next__()
    print(item)
```

As you can see, the *for-in* was just syntactic sugar for a simple while loop:

- It first prepared the repeater object for iteration by calling its __iter__ method. This returned the actual *iterator object*.
- After that, the loop repeatedly called the iterator object's __next__ method to retrieve values from it.

If you've ever worked with *database cursors*, this mental model will seem familiar: We first initialize the cursor and prepare it for reading, and then we can fetch data from it into local variables as needed, one element at a time.

Because there's never more than one element "in flight," this approach is highly memory-efficient. Our Repeater class provides an *infinite* sequence of elements and we can iterate over it just fine. Emulating the same thing with a Python list would be impossible—there's no way we could create a list with an infinite number of elements in the first place. This makes iterators a very powerful concept.

On more abstract terms, iterators provide a common interface that allows you to process every element of a container while being completely isolated from the container's internal structure.

Whether you're dealing with a list of elements, a dictionary, an infinite sequence like the one provided by our Repeater class, or another sequence type—all of that is just an implementation detail. Every single one of these objects can be traversed in the same way with the power of iterators.

And as you've seen, there's nothing special about *for-in* loops in Python. If you peek behind the curtain, it all comes down to calling the right dunder methods at the right time.

In fact, you can manually "emulate" how the loop uses the iterator protocol in a Python interpreter session:

```
>>> repeater = Repeater('Hello')
>>> iterator = iter(repeater)
>>> next(iterator)
'Hello'
>>> next(iterator)
'Hello'
>>> next(iterator)
'Hello'
...
```

This gives the same result—an infinite stream of hellos. Every time you call next(), the iterator hands out the same greeting again.

By the way, I took the opportunity here to replace the calls to __iter__ and __next__ with calls to Python's built-in functions, iter() and next().

Internally, these built-ins invoke the same dunder methods, but they make this code a little prettier and easier to read by providing a clean "facade" to the iterator protocol.

Python offers these facades for other functionality as well. For example, len(x) is a shortcut for calling x.__len__. Similarly, calling iter(x) invokes x.__iter__ and calling next(x) invokes x.__next__.

Generally, it's a good idea to use the built-in facade functions rather than directly accessing the dunder methods implementing a protocol. It just makes the code a little easier to read.

A Simpler Iterator Class

Up until now, our iterator example consisted of two separate classes, Repeater and RepeaterIterator. They corresponded directly to the two phases used by Python's iterator protocol:

First, setting up and retrieving the iterator object with an iter() call, and then repeatedly fetching values from it via next().

Many times *both of these responsibilities* can be shouldered by a single class. Doing this allows you to reduce the amount of code necessary to write a class-based iterator.

I chose not to do this with the first example in this chapter because it mixes up the cleanliness of the mental model behind the iterator protocol. But now that you've seen how to write a class-based iterator the longer and more complicated way, let's take a minute to simplify what we've got so far.

Remember why we needed the RepeaterIterator class again? We needed it to host the __next__ method for fetching new values from the iterator. But it doesn't really matter *where* __next__ is defined. In the iterator protocol, all that matters is that __iter__ returns *any* object with a __next__ method on it.

So here's an idea: RepeaterIterator returns the same value over and over, and it doesn't have to keep track of any internal state. What if we added the __next__ method directly to the Repeater class instead?

That way we could get rid of RepeaterIterator altogether and implement an iterable object with a single Python class. Let's try it out! Our new and simplified iterator example looks as follows:

```python
class Repeater:
    def __init__(self, value):
        self.value = value

    def __iter__(self):
        return self

    def __next__(self):
        return self.value
```

We just went from two separate classes and 10 lines of code to just one class and 7 lines of code. Our simplified implementation still supports the iterator protocol just fine:

```python
>>> repeater = Repeater('Hello')
>>> for item in repeater:
...     print(item)

Hello
Hello
Hello
...
```

Streamlining a class-based iterator like that often makes sense. In fact, most Python iterator tutorials start out that way. But I always felt that explaining iterators with a single class from the get-go hides the underlying principles of the iterator protocol—and thus makes it more difficult to understand.

Who Wants to Iterate Forever

At this point you should have a pretty good understanding of how iterators work in Python. But so far we've only implemented iterators that keep on iterating *forever*.

Clearly, infinite repetition isn't the main use case for iterators in Python. In fact, when you look back all the way to the beginning of this chapter, I used the following snippet as a motivating example:

```
numbers = [1, 2, 3]
for n in numbers:
    print(n)
```

You'll rightfully expect this code to print the numbers 1, 2, and 3 and then stop. And you probably *wouldn't* expect it to go on spamming your terminal window by printing "3" forever until you mash *Ctrl+C* a few times in a wild panic...

And so, it's time to find out how to write an iterator that eventually *stops* generating new values instead of iterating forever because that's what Python objects typically do when we use them in a *for-in* loop.

We'll now write another iterator class that we'll call `BoundedRepeater`. It'll be similar to our previous `Repeater` example, but this time we'll want it to stop after a predefined number of repetitions.

Let's think about this for a bit. How do we do this? How does an iterator signal that it's exhausted and out of elements to iterate over? Maybe you're thinking, "Hmm, we could just return None from the __next__ method."

And that's not a bad idea—but the trouble is, what are we going to do if we *want* some iterators to be able to return None as an acceptable value?

Let's see what other Python iterators do to solve this problem. I'm going to construct a simple container, a list with a few elements, and then I'll iterate over it until it runs out of elements to see what happens:

```
>>> my_list = [1, 2, 3]
>>> iterator = iter(my_list)
```

```
>>> next(iterator)
1
>>> next(iterator)
2
>>> next(iterator)
3
```

Careful now! We've consumed all of the three available elements in the list. Watch what happens if I call next on the iterator again:

```
>>> next(iterator)
StopIteration
```

Aha! It raises a StopIteration exception to signal we've exhausted all of the available values in the iterator.

That's right: Iterators use exceptions to structure control flow. To signal the end of iteration, a Python iterator simply raises the built-in StopIteration exception.

If I keep requesting more values from the iterator, it'll keep raising StopIteration exceptions to signal that there are no more values available to iterate over:

```
>>> next(iterator)
StopIteration
>>> next(iterator)
StopIteration
...
```

Python iterators normally can't be "reset"—once they're exhausted they're supposed to raise StopIteration every time next() is called on them. To iterate anew you'll need to request a fresh iterator object with the iter() function.

Now we know everything we need to write our BoundedRepeater class
that stops iterating after a set number of repetitions:

```python
class BoundedRepeater:
    def __init__(self, value, max_repeats):
        self.value = value
        self.max_repeats = max_repeats
        self.count = 0

    def __iter__(self):
        return self

    def __next__(self):
        if self.count >= self.max_repeats:
            raise StopIteration
        self.count += 1
        return self.value
```

This gives us the desired result. Iteration stops after the number of
repetitions defined in the max_repeats parameter:

```python
>>> repeater = BoundedRepeater('Hello', 3)
>>> for item in repeater:
        print(item)
Hello
Hello
Hello
```

If we rewrite this last for-in loop example to take away some of the
syntactic sugar, we end up with the following expanded code snippet:

```python
repeater = BoundedRepeater('Hello', 3)
iterator = iter(repeater)
while True:
    try:
```

```
    item = next(iterator)
except StopIteration:
    break
print(item)
```

Every time next() is called in this loop, we check for a StopIteration exception and break the while loop if necessary.

Being able to write a three-line *for-in* loop instead of an eight-line while loop is quite a nice improvement. It makes the code easier to read and more maintainable. And this is another reason why iterators in Python are such a powerful tool.

Python 2.x Compatibility

All the code examples I showed here were written in Python 3. There's a small but important difference between Python 2 and 3 when it comes to implementing class-based iterators:

- In Python 3, the method that retrieves the next value from an iterator is called __next__.
- In Python 2, the same method is called next (no underscores).

This naming difference can lead to some trouble if you're trying to write class-based iterators that should work on both versions of Python. Luckily, there's a simple approach you can take to work around this difference.

Here's an updated version of the InfiniteRepeater class that will work on both Python 2 and Python 3:

```
class InfiniteRepeater(object):
    def __init__(self, value):
        self.value = value
```

```
def __iter__(self):
    return self

def __next__(self):
    return self.value

# Python 2 compatibility:
def next(self):
    return self.__next__()
```

To make this iterator class compatible with Python 2, I've made two small changes to it:

First, I added a next method that simply calls the original __next__ and forwards its return value. This essentially creates an alias for the existing __next__ implementation so that Python 2 finds it. That way we can support both versions of Python while still keeping all of the actual implementation details in one place.

And second, I modified the class definition to inherit from object in order to ensure we're creating a *new-style* class on Python 2. This has nothing to do with iterators specifically, but it's a good practice nonetheless.

Key Takeaways

- Iterators provide a sequence interface to Python objects that's memory efficient and considered Pythonic. Behold the beauty of the *for-in* loop!
- To support iteration an object needs to implement the *iterator protocol* by providing the __iter__ and __next__ dunder methods.
- Class-based iterators are only one way to write iterable objects in Python. Also consider generators and generator expressions.

6.5 Generators Are Simplified Iterators

In the chapter on iterators we spent quite a bit of time writing a class-based iterator. This wasn't a bad idea from an educational perspective—but it also demonstrated how writing an iterator class requires a lot of boilerplate code. To tell you the truth, as a "lazy" developer, I don't like tedious and repetitive work.

And yet, iterators are so useful in Python. They allow you to write pretty *for-in* loops and help you make your code more Pythonic and efficient. If there only was a more convenient way to write these iterators in the first place...

Surprise, there is! Once more, Python helps us out with some syntactic sugar to make writing iterators easier. In this chapter you'll see how to write iterators faster and with less code using *generators* and the `yield` keyword.

Infinite Generators

Let's start by looking again at the Repeater example that I previously used to introduce the idea of iterators. It implemented a class-based iterator cycling through an infinite sequence of values. This is what the class looked like in its second (simplified) version:

```
class Repeater:
    def __init__(self, value):
        self.value = value

    def __iter__(self):
        return self

    def __next__(self):
        return self.value
```

If you're thinking, "that's quite a lot of code for such a simple iterator," you're absolutely right. Parts of this class seem rather formulaic, as if they would be written in exactly the same way from one class-based iterator to the next.

This is where Python's *generators* enter the scene. If I rewrite this iterator class as a generator, it looks like this:

```python
def repeater(value):
    while True:
        yield value
```

We just went from seven lines of code to three. Not bad, eh? As you can see, generators look like regular functions but instead of using the return statement, they use yield to pass data back to the caller.

Will this new generator implementation still work the same way as our class-based iterator did? Let's bust out the *for-in* loop test to find out:

```python
>>> for x in repeater('Hi'):
...     print(x)
'Hi'
'Hi'
'Hi'
'Hi'
'Hi'
...
```

Yep! We're still looping through our greetings forever. This much shorter *generator* implementation seems to perform the same way that the Repeater class did. (Remember to hit *Ctrl+C* if you want out of the infinite loop in an interpreter session.)

Now, how do these generators work? They look like normal functions, but their behavior is quite different. For starters, calling a generator function doesn't even run the function. It merely creates and returns a *generator object*:

```
>>> repeater('Hey')
<generator object repeater at 0x107bcdbf8>
```

The code in the generator function only executes when `next()` is called on the generator object:

```
>>> generator_obj = repeater('Hey')
>>> next(generator_obj)
'Hey'
```

If you read the code of the `repeater` function again, it looks like the `yield` keyword in there somehow stops this generator function in mid-execution and then resumes it at a later point in time:

```
def repeater(value):
    while True:
        yield value
```

And that's quite a fitting mental model for what happens here. You see, when a `return` statement is invoked inside a function, it permanently passes control back to the caller of the function. When a `yield` is invoked, it also passes control back to the caller of the function—but it only does so *temporarily*.

Whereas a `return` statement disposes of a function's local state, a `yield` statement suspends the function and retains its local state. In practical terms, this means local variables and the execution state of the generator function are only stashed away temporarily and not thrown out completely. Execution can be resumed at any time by calling `next()` on the generator:

```
>>> iterator = repeater('Hi')
>>> next(iterator)
'Hi'
```

```
>>> next(iterator)
'Hi'
>>> next(iterator)
'Hi'
```

This makes generators fully compatible with the iterator protocol. For this reason, I like to think of them primarily as syntactic sugar for implementing iterators.

You'll find that for most types of iterators, writing a generator function will be easier and more readable than defining a long-winded class-based iterator.

Generators That Stop Generating

In this chapter we started out by writing an *infinite* generator once again. By now you're probably wondering how to write a generator that stops producing values after a while, instead of going on and on forever.

Remember, in our class-based iterator we were able to signal the end of iteration by manually raising a StopIteration exception. Because generators are fully compatible with class-based iterators, that's still what happens behind the scenes.

Thankfully, as programmers we get to work with a nicer interface this time around. Generators stop generating values as soon as control flow returns from the generator function by any means other than a yield statement. This means you no longer have to worry about raising StopIteration at all!

Here's an example:

```
def repeat_three_times(value):
    yield value
    yield value
    yield value
```

Notice how this generator function doesn't include any kind of loop. In fact it's dead simple and only consists of three `yield` statements. If a `yield` temporarily suspends execution of the function and passes back a value to the caller, what will happen when we reach the end of this generator? Let's find out:

```
>>> for x in repeat_three_times('Hey there'):
...         print(x)
'Hey there'
'Hey there'
'Hey there'
```

As you may have expected, this generator stopped producing new values after three iterations. We can assume that it did so by raising a `StopIteration` exception when execution reached the end of the function. But to be sure, let's confirm that with another experiment:

```
>>> iterator = repeat_three_times('Hey there')
>>> next(iterator)
'Hey there'
>>> next(iterator)
'Hey there'
>>> next(iterator)
'Hey there'
>>> next(iterator)
StopIteration
>>> next(iterator)
StopIteration
```

This iterator behaved just like we expected. As soon as we reach the end of the generator function, it keeps raising `StopIteration` to signal that it has no more values to provide.

Let's come back to another example from the iterators chapter. The `BoundedIterator` class implemented an iterator that would only repeat a value a set number of times:

```python
class BoundedRepeater:
    def __init__(self, value, max_repeats):
        self.value = value
        self.max_repeats = max_repeats
        self.count = 0

    def __iter__(self):
        return self

    def __next__(self):
        if self.count >= self.max_repeats:
            raise StopIteration
        self.count += 1
        return self.value
```

Why don't we try to re-implement this `BoundedRepeater` class as a generator function. Here's my first take on it:

```python
def bounded_repeater(value, max_repeats):
    count = 0
    while True:
        if count >= max_repeats:
            return
        count += 1
        yield value
```

I intentionally made the `while` loop in this function a little unwieldy. I wanted to demonstrate how invoking a `return` statement from a generator causes iteration to stop with a `StopIteration` exception. We'll soon clean up and simplify this generator function some more, but first let's try out what we've got so far:

```python
>>> for x in bounded_repeater('Hi', 4):
...     print(x)
'Hi'
```

```
'Hi'
'Hi'
'Hi'
```

Great! Now we have a generator that stops producing values after a configurable number of repetitions. It uses the `yield` statement to pass back values until it finally hits the `return` statement and iteration stops.

Like I promised you, we can further simplify this generator. We'll take advantage of the fact that Python adds an implicit `return None` statement to the end of every function. This is what our final implementation looks like:

```python
def bounded_repeater(value, max_repeats):
    for i in range(max_repeats):
        yield value
```

Feel free to confirm that this simplified generator still works the same way. All things considered, we went from a 12-line implementation in the `BoundedRepeater` class to a three-line generator-based implementation providing the exact same functionality. That's a 75% reduction in the number of lines of code—not too shabby!

As you just saw, generators help "abstract away" most of the boilerplate code otherwise needed when writing class-based iterators. They can make your life as a programmer much easier and allow you to write cleaner, shorter, and more maintainable iterators. Generator functions are a great feature in Python, and you shouldn't hesitate to use them in your own programs.

Key Takeaways

- Generator functions are syntactic sugar for writing objects that support the iterator protocol. Generators abstract away much

of the boilerplate code needed when writing class-based iterators.

- The `yield` statement allows you to temporarily suspend execution of a generator function and to pass back values from it.
- Generators start raising `StopIteration` exceptions after control flow leaves the generator function by any means other than
  a `yield` statement.

6.6 Generator Expressions

As I learned more about Python's iterator protocol and the different ways to implement it in my own code, I realized that "syntactic sugar" was a recurring theme.

You see, class-based iterators and generator functions are two expressions of the same underlying design pattern.

Generator functions give you a shortcut for supporting the iterator protocol in your own code, and they avoid much of the verbosity of class-based iterators. With a little bit of specialized syntax, or *syntactic sugar*, they save you time and make your life as a developer easier.

This is a recurring theme in Python and in other programming languages. As more developers use a design pattern in their programs, there's a growing incentive for the language creators to provide abstractions and implementation shortcuts for it.

That's how programming languages evolve over time—and as developers, we reap the benefits. We get to work with more and more powerful building blocks, which reduces busywork and lets us achieve more in less time.

Earlier in this book you saw how generators provide syntactic sugar for writing class-based iterators. The *generator expressions* we'll cover in this chapter add another layer of syntactic sugar on top.

Generator expressions give you an even more effective shortcut for writing iterators. With a simple and concise syntax that looks like a list comprehension, you'll be able to define iterators in a single line of code.

Here's an example:

```
iterator = ('Hello' for i in range(3))
```

When iterated over, this generator expression yields the same sequence of values as the bounded_repeater generator function we wrote in the previous chapter. Here it is again to refresh your memory:

```
def bounded_repeater(value, max_repeats):
    for i in range(max_repeats):
        yield value

iterator = bounded_repeater('Hello', 3)
```

Isn't it amazing how a single-line generator expression now does a job that previously required a four-line generator function or a much longer class-based iterator?

But I'm getting ahead of myself. Let's make sure our iterator defined with a generator expression actually works as expected:

```
>>> iterator = ('Hello' for i in range(3))
>>> for x in iterator:
...     print(x)
'Hello'
'Hello'
'Hello'
```

That looks pretty good to me! We seem to get the same results from our one-line generator expression that we got from the bounded_repeater generator function.

There's one small caveat though: Once a generator expression has been consumed, it can't be restarted or reused. So in some cases there is an advantage to using generator functions or class-based iterators.

Generator Expressions vs List Comprehensions

As you can tell, generator expressions are somewhat similar to list comprehensions:

```
>>> listcomp = ['Hello' for i in range(3)]
>>> genexpr = ('Hello' for i in range(3))
```

Unlike list comprehensions, however, generator expressions don't construct list objects. Instead, they generate values "just in time" like a class-based iterator or generator function would.

All you get by assigning a generator expression to a variable is an iterable "generator object":

```
>>> listcomp
['Hello', 'Hello', 'Hello']

>>> genexpr
<generator object <genexpr> at 0x1036c3200>
```

To access the values produced by the generator expression, you need to call next() on it, just like you would with any other iterator:

```
>>> next(genexpr)
'Hello'
>>> next(genexpr)
'Hello'
>>> next(genexpr)
'Hello'
>>> next(genexpr)
StopIteration
```

Alternatively, you can also call the list() function on a generator expression to construct a list object holding all generated values:

```
>>> genexpr = ('Hello' for i in range(3))
>>> list(genexpr)
['Hello', 'Hello', 'Hello']
```

Of course, this was just a toy example to show how you can "convert" a generator expression (or any other iterator for that matter) into a list. If you need a list object right away, you'd normally just write a list comprehension from the get-go.

Let's take a closer look at the syntactic structure of this simple generator expression. The pattern you should begin to see looks like this:

```
genexpr = (expression for item in collection)
```

The above generator expression "template" corresponds to the following generator function:

```
def generator():
    for item in collection:
        yield expression
```

Just like with list comprehensions, this gives you a "cookie-cutter pattern" you can apply to many generator functions in order to transform them into concise *generator expressions*.

Filtering Values

There's one more useful addition we can make to this template, and that's element filtering with conditions. Here's an example:

```
>>> even_squares = (x * x for x in range(10)
                    if x % 2 == 0)
```

This generator yields the square numbers of all even integers from zero to nine. The filtering condition using the % (modulo) operator will reject any value not divisible by two:

```
>>> for x in even_squares:
...     print(x)
0
4
16
36
64
```

Let's update our generator expression template. After adding element filtering via if-conditions, the template now looks like this:

```
genexpr = (expression for item in collection
           if condition)
```

And once again, this pattern corresponds to a relatively straightforward, but longer, generator function. Syntactic sugar at its best:

```
def generator():
    for item in collection:
        if condition:
            yield expression
```

In-line Generator Expressions

Because generator expressions are, well...expressions, you can use them in-line with other statements. For example, you can define an iterator and consume it right away with a for-loop:

```
for x in ('Bom dia' for i in range(3)):
    print(x)
```

There's another syntactic trick you can use to make your generator expressions more beautiful. The parentheses surrounding a generator expression can be dropped if the generator expression is used as the single argument to a function:

```
>>> sum((x * 2 for x in range(10)))
90

# Versus:

>>> sum(x * 2 for x in range(10))
90
```

This allows you to write concise and performant code. Because generator expressions generate values "just in time" like a class-based iterator or a generator function would, they are very memory efficient.

Too Much of a Good Thing...

Like list comprehensions, generator expressions allow for more complexity than what we've covered so far. Through nested for-loops and chained filtering clauses, they can cover a wider range of use cases:

```
(expr for x in xs if cond1
      for y in ys if cond2
      ...
      for z in zs if condN)
```

The above pattern translates to the following generator function logic:

```
for x in xs:
    if cond1:
        for y in ys:
            if cond2:
                ...
                    for z in zs:
                        if condN:
                            yield expr
```

And this is where I'd like to place a big caveat:

Please don't write deeply nested generator expressions like that. They can be very difficult to maintain in the long run.

This is one of those "the dose makes the poison" situations where a beautiful and simple tool can be overused to create hard to read and difficult to debug programs.

Just like with list comprehensions, I personally try to stay away from any generator expression that includes more than two levels of nesting.

Generator expressions are a helpful and Pythonic tool in your toolbox, but that doesn't mean they should be used for every single problem you're facing. For complex iterators, it's often better to write a generator function or even a class-based iterator.

If you need to use nested generators and complex filtering conditions, it's usually better to factor out sub-generators (so you can name them) and then to chain them together again at the top level. You'll see how to do this in the next chapter on *iterator chains*.

If you're on the fence, try out different implementations and then select the one that seems the most readable. Trust me, it'll save you time in the long run.

Key Takeaways

- Generator expressions are similar to list comprehensions. However, they don't construct list objects. Instead, generator expressions generate values "just in time" like a class-based iterator or generator function would.
- Once a generator expression has been consumed, it can't be restarted or reused.
- Generator expressions are best for implementing simple "ad hoc" iterators. For complex iterators, it's better to write a generator function or a class-based iterator.

6.7 Iterator Chains

Here's another great feature of iterators in Python: By chaining together multiple iterators you can write highly efficient data processing "pipelines." The first time I saw this pattern in action in a PyCon presentation by David Beazley, it blew my mind.

If you take advantage of Python's generator functions and generator expressions, you'll be building concise and powerful *iterator chains* in no time. In this chapter you'll find out what this technique looks like in practice and how you can use it in your own programs.

As a quick recap, generators and generator expressions are syntactic sugar for writing iterators in Python. They abstract away much of the boilerplate code needed when writing class-based iterators.

While a regular function produces a single return value, generators produce a sequence of results. You could say they *generate a stream of values* over the course of their lifetime.

For example, I can define the following generator that produces the series of integer values from one to eight by keeping a running counter and yielding a new value every time next() gets called on it:

```python
def integers():
    for i in range(1, 9):
        yield i
```

You can confirm this behaviour by running the following code in a Python REPL:

```python
>>> chain = integers()
>>> list(chain)
[1, 2, 3, 4, 5, 6, 7, 8]
```

So far, so not-very-interesting. But we'll quickly change this now. You see, generators can be "connected" to each other in order to build efficient data processing algorithms that work like a pipeline.

You can take the "stream" of values coming out of the `integers()` generator and feed them into another generator again. For example, one that takes each number, squares it, and then passes it on:

```python
def squared(seq):
    for i in seq:
        yield i * i
```

This is what our "data pipeline" or "chain of generators" would do now:

```python
>>> chain = squared(integers())
>>> list(chain)
[1, 4, 9, 16, 25, 36, 49, 64]
```

And we can keep on adding new building blocks to this pipeline. Data flows in one direction only, and each processing step is shielded from the others via a well-defined interface.

This is similar to how pipelines work in Unix. We chain together a sequence of processes so that the output of each process feeds directly as input to the next one.

Why don't we add another step to our pipeline that negates each value and then passes it on to the next processing step in the chain:

```python
def negated(seq):
    for i in seq:
        yield -i
```

If we rebuild our chain of generators and add `negated` at the end, this is the output we get now:

```
>>> chain = negated(squared(integers()))
>>> list(chain)
[-1, -4, -9, -16, -25, -36, -49, -64]
```

My favorite thing about chaining generators is that the data process-ing happens *one element at a time*. There's no buffering between the processing steps in the chain:

1. The `integers` generator yields a single value, let's say 3.
2. This "activates" the `squared` generator, which processes the value and passes it on to the next stage as 3 × 3 = 9
3. The square number yielded by the `squared` generator gets fed immediately into the `negated` generator, which modifies it to -9 and yields it again.

You could keep extending this chain of generators to build out a pro-cessing pipeline with many steps. It would still perform efficiently and could easily be modified because each step in the chain is an individ-ual generator function.

Each individual generator function in this processing pipeline is quite concise. With a little trick, we can shrink down the definition of this pipeline even more, without sacrificing much readability:

```
integers = range(8)
squared = (i * i for i in integers)
negated = (-i for i in squared)
```

Notice how I've replaced each processing step in the chain with a *gen-erator expression* built on the output of the previous step. This code is equivalent to the chain of generators we built throughout the chapter:

```
>>> negated
<generator object <genexpr> at 0x1098bcb48>
>>> list(negated)
[0, -1, -4, -9, -16, -25, -36, -49]
```

The only downside to using generator expressions is that they can't be configured with function arguments, and you can't reuse the same generator expression multiple times in the same processing pipeline.

But of course, you could mix-and-match generator expressions and regular generators freely in building these pipelines. This will help improve readability with complex pipelines.

Key Takeaways

- Generators can be chained together to form highly efficient and maintainable data processing pipelines.
- Chained generators process each element going through the chain individually.
- Generator expressions can be used to write concise pipeline definitions, but this can impact readability.

Chapter 7

Dictionary Tricks

7.1 Dictionary Default Values

Python's dictionaries have a get() method for looking up a key while providing a fallback value. This can be handy in many situations. Let me give you a simple example to show you what I mean. Imagine we have the following data structure that's mapping user IDs to user names:

```
name_for_userid = {
    382: 'Alice',
    950: 'Bob',
    590: 'Dilbert',
}
```

Now we'd like to use this data structure to write a function greeting() which will return a greeting for a user based on their user ID. Our first implementation might look something like this:

```
def greeting(userid):
    return 'Hi %s!' % name_for_userid[userid]
```

It's a straightforward dictionary lookup. This first implementation technically works—but only if the user ID is a valid key in the name_for_userid dictionary. If we pass an *invalid* user ID to our greeting function it throws an exception:

```
>>> greeting(382)
'Hi Alice!'

>>> greeting(33333333)
KeyError: 33333333
```

A KeyError exception isn't really the result we'd like to see. It would be much nicer if the function returned a generic greeting as a fallback if the user ID can't be found.

Let's implement this idea. Our first approach might be to simply do a *key in dict* membership check and to return a default greeting if the user ID is unknown:

```python
def greeting(userid):
    if userid in name_for_userid:
        return 'Hi %s!' % name_for_userid[userid]
    else:
        return 'Hi there!'
```

Let's see how this implementation of `greeting()` fares with our previous test cases:

```python
>>> greeting(382)
'Hi Alice!'

>>> greeting(33333333)
'Hi there!'
```

Much better. We now get a generic greeting for unknown users and we keep the personalized greeting when a valid user ID is found.

But there's still room for improvement. While this new implementation gives us the expected results and seems small and clean enough, it can still be improved. I've got some gripes with the current approach:

- It's *inefficient* because it queries the dictionary twice.

- It's *verbose* since part of the greeting string is repeated, for example.

- It's not *Pythonic*—the official Python documentation specifically recommends an "easier to ask for forgiveness than permission" (EAFP) coding style for these situations:

255

"This common Python coding style assumes the existence of valid keys or attributes and catches exceptions if the assumption proves false."[1]

A better implementation that follows the *EAFP* principle might use a *try...except* block to catch the KeyError instead of doing an explicit membership test:

```python
def greeting(userid):
    try:
        return 'Hi %s!' % name_for_userid[userid]
    except KeyError:
        return 'Hi there'
```

This implementation is still correct as far as our initial requirements go, and now we've removed the need for querying the dictionary twice.

But we can still improve this further and come up with a cleaner solution. Python's dictionaries have a get() method on them which supports a "default" parameter that can be used as a fallback value:[2]

```python
def greeting(userid):
    return 'Hi %s!' % name_for_userid.get(
        userid, 'there')
```

When get() is called, it checks if the given key exists in the dictionary. If it does, the value for the key is returned. If it does *not* exist, then the value of the default parameter is returned instead. As you can see, this implementation of greeting still works as intended:

```python
>>> greeting(950)
'Hi Bob!'
```

---

[1]cf. Python Glossary: "EAFP"
[2]cf. Python Docs: dict.get() method

```
>>> greeting(333333)
'Hi there!'
```

Our final implementation of greeting() is concise, clean, and only uses features from the Python standard library. Therefore, I believe it is the best solution for this particular situation.

Key Takeaways

- Avoid explicit *key in dict* checks when testing for membership.
- EAFP-style exception handling or using the built-in get() method is preferable.
- In some cases, the collections.defaultdict class from the standard library can also be helpful.

7.2 Sorting Dictionaries for Fun and Profit

Python dictionaries don't have an inherent order. You can iterate over them just fine but there's no guarantee that iteration returns the dictionary's elements in any particular order (although this is changing with Python 3.6).

However, it's frequently useful to get a *sorted representation* of a dictionary to put the dictionary's items into an arbitrary order based on their key, value, or some other derived property. Suppose you have a dictionary xs with the following key/value pairs:

```
>>> xs = {'a': 4, 'c': 2, 'b': 3, 'd': 1}
```

To get a sorted list of the key/value pairs in this dictionary, you could use the dictionary's `items()` method and then sort the resulting sequence in a second pass:

```
>>> sorted(xs.items())
[('a', 4), ('b', 3), ('c', 2), ('d', 1)]
```

The key/value tuples are ordered using Python's standard lexicographical ordering for comparing sequences.

To compare two tuples, Python compares the items stored at index zero first. If they differ, this defines the outcome of the comparison. If they're equal, the next two items at index one are compared, and so on.

Now, because we took these tuples from a dictionary, all of the former dictionary keys at index zero in each tuple are unique. Therefore, there are no ties to break here.

In some cases a lexicographical ordering might be exactly what you want. In other cases you might want to sort a dictionary by value instead.

Luckily, there's a way you can get complete control over how items are ordered. You can control the ordering by passing a *key func* to sorted() that will change how dictionary items are compared.

A *key func* is simply a normal Python function to be called on each element prior to making comparisons. The key func gets a dictionary item as its input and returns the desired "key" for the sort order comparisons.

Unfortunately, the word "key" is used in two contexts simultaneously here—the key func doesn't deal with dictionary keys, it merely maps each input item to an arbitrary *comparison key*.

Now, maybe we should look at an example. Trust me, key funcs will be much easier to understand once you see some real code.

Let's say you wanted to get a sorted representation of a dictionary based on its *values*. To get this result you could use the following key func which returns the value of each key/value pair by looking up the second element in the tuple:

```
>>> sorted(xs.items(), key=lambda x: x[1])
[('d', 1), ('c', 2), ('b', 3), ('a', 4)]
```

See how the resulting list of key/value pairs is now sorted by the values stored in the original dictionary? It's worth spending some time wrapping your head around how key funcs work. It's a powerful concept that you can apply in all kinds of Python contexts.

In fact, the concept is so common that Python's standard library includes the operator module. This module implements some of the most frequently used key funcs as plug-and-play building blocks, like operator.itemgetter and operator.attrgetter.

Here's an example of how you might replace the lambda-based index lookup in the first example with operator.itemgetter:

```
>>> import operator
>>> sorted(xs.items(), key=operator.itemgetter(1))
[('d', 1), ('c', 2), ('b', 3), ('a', 4)]
```

Using the operator module might communicate your code's intent more clearly in some cases. On the other hand, using a simple lambda expression might be just as readable and more explicit. In this particular case, I actually prefer the lambda expression.

Another benefit of using lambdas as a custom key func is that you get to control the sort order in much finer detail. For example, you could sort a dictionary based on the absolute numeric value of each value stored in it:

```
>>> sorted(xs.items(), key=lambda x: abs(x[1]))
```

If you need to reverse the sort order so that larger values go first, you can use the reverse=True keyword argument when calling sorted():

```
>>> sorted(xs.items(),
           key=lambda x: x[1],
           reverse=True)
[('a', 4), ('b', 3), ('c', 2), ('d', 1)]
```

Like I said earlier, it's totally worth spending some time getting a good grip on how key funcs work in Python. They provide you with a ton of flexibility and can often save you from writing code to transform one data structure into another.

Key Takeaways

- When creating sorted "views" of dictionaries and other collections, you can influence the sort order with a *key func*.

- *Key funcs* are an important concept in Python. The most frequently used ones were even added to the operator module in the standard library.
- Functions are first-class citizens in Python. This is a powerful feature you'll find used everywhere in the language.

7.3 Emulating Switch/Case Statements With Dicts

Python doesn't have switch/case statements so it's sometimes necessary to write long if...elif...else chains as a workaround. In this chapter you'll discover a trick you can use to emulate switch/case statements in Python with dictionaries and first-class functions. Sound exciting? Great—here we go!

Imagine we had the following if-chain in our program:

```
>>> if cond == 'cond_a':
...     handle_a()
... elif cond == 'cond_b':
...     handle_b()
... else:
...     handle_default()
```

Of course, with only three different conditions, this isn't too horrible yet. But just imagine if we had ten or more elif branches in this statement. Things would start to look a little different. I consider long if-chains to be a *code smell* that makes programs more difficult to read and maintain.

One way to deal with long if...elif...else statements is to replace them with dictionary lookup tables that emulate the behavior of switch/case statements.

The idea here is to leverage the fact that Python has *first-class functions*. This means they can be passed as arguments to other functions, returned as values from other functions, and assigned to variables and stored in data structures.

For example, we can define a function and then store it in a list for later access:

```
>>> def myfunc(a, b):
...     return a + b
...
>>> funcs = [myfunc]
>>> funcs[0]
<function myfunc at 0x107012230>
```

The syntax for calling this function works as you'd intuitively expect—
we simply use an index into the list and then use the "()" call syntax
for calling the function and passing arguments to it:

```
>>> funcs[0](2, 3)
5
```

Now, how are we going to use first-class functions to cut our chained
if-statement back to size? The core idea here is to define a dictionary
that maps lookup keys for the input conditions to functions that will
carry out the intended operations:

```
>>> func_dict = {
...     'cond_a': handle_a,
...     'cond_b': handle_b
... }
```

Instead of filtering through the if-statement, checking each condition
as we go along, we can do a dictionary key lookup to get the handler
function and then call it:

```
>>> cond = 'cond_a'
>>> func_dict[cond]()
```

This implementation already sort-of works, at least as long as cond
can be found in the dictionary. If it's not in there, we'll get a KeyError
exception.

So let's look for a way to support a *default* case that would match the original `else` branch. Luckily all Python dicts have a `get()` method on them that returns the value for a given key, or a default value if the key can't be found. This is exactly what we need here:

```
>>> func_dict.get(cond, handle_default)()
```

This code snippet might look syntactically odd at first, but when you break it down, it works exactly like the earlier example. Again, we're using Python's first-class functions to pass `handle_default` to the `get()`-lookup as a fallback value. That way, if the condition can't be found in the dictionary, we avoid raising a `KeyError` and call the default handler function instead.

Let's take a look at a more complete example for using dictionary lookups and first-class functions to replace `if`-chains. After reading through the following example, you'll be able to see the pattern needed to transform certain kinds of `if`-statements to a dictionary-based dispatch.

We're going to write another function with an `if`-chain that we'll then transform. The function takes a string opcode like `"add"` or `"mul"` and then does some math on the operands x and y:

```
>>> def dispatch_if(operator, x, y):
...     if operator == 'add':
...         return x + y
...     elif operator == 'sub':
...         return x - y
...     elif operator == 'mul':
...         return x * y
...     elif operator == 'div':
...         return x / y
```

To be honest, this is yet another toy example (I don't want to bore you with pages and pages of code here), but it'll serve well to illustrate the underlying design pattern. Once you "get" the pattern, you'll be able to apply it in all kinds of different scenarios.

You can try out this dispatch_if() function to perform simple calculations by calling the function with a string opcode and two numeric operands:

```
>>> dispatch_if('mul', 2, 8)
16
>>> dispatch_if('unknown', 2, 8)
None
```

Please note that the 'unknown' case works because Python adds an implicit return None statement to the end of any function.

So far so good. Let's transform the original dispatch_if() into a new function which uses a dictionary to map opcodes to arithmetic operations with first-class functions.

```
>>> def dispatch_dict(operator, x, y):
...     return {
...         'add': lambda: x + y,
...         'sub': lambda: x - y,
...         'mul': lambda: x * y,
...         'div': lambda: x / y,
...     }.get(operator, lambda: None)()
```

This dictionary-based implementation gives the same results as the original dispatch_if(). We can call both functions in exactly the same way:

```
>>> dispatch_dict('mul', 2, 8)
16
>>> dispatch_dict('unknown', 2, 8)
None
```

There are a couple of ways this code could be further improved if it was real "production-grade" code.

First of all, every time we call `dispatch_dict()`, it creates a temporary dictionary and a bunch of lambdas for the opcode lookup. This isn't ideal from a performance perspective. For code that needs to be fast, it makes more sense to create the dictionary once as a constant and then to reference it when the function is called. We don't want to recreate the dictionary every time we need to do a lookup.

Second, if we really wanted to do some simple arithmetic like x + y, then we'd be better off using Python's built-in `operator` module instead of the lambda functions used in the example. The `operator` module provides implementations for all of Python's operators, for example `operator.mul`, `operator.div`, and so on. This is a minor point, though. I intentionally used lambdas in this example to make it more generic. This should help you apply the pattern in other situations as well.

Well, now you've got another tool in your bag of tricks that you can use to simplify some of your `if`-chains should they get unwieldy. Just remember—this technique won't apply in every situation and sometimes you'll be better off with a plain `if`-statement.

Key Takeaways

- Python doesn't have a switch/case statement. But in some cases you can avoid long `if`-chains with a dictionary-based dispatch table.
- Once again Python's first-class functions prove to be a powerful tool. But with great power comes great responsibility.

7.4 The Craziest Dict Expression in the West

Sometimes you strike upon a tiny code example that has real depth to it—a single line of code that can teach you a lot about a programming language if you ponder it enough. Such a code snippet feels like a *Zen kōan*: a question or statement used in Zen practice to provoke doubt and test the student's progress.

The tiny little code snippet we'll discuss in this chapter is one such example. Upon first glance, it might seem like a straightforward dictionary expression, but when considered at close range, it takes you on a mind-expanding journey through the CPython interpreter.

I get such a kick out of this little one-liner that at one point I had it printed on my Python conference badges as a conversation starter. It also led to some rewarding conversations with members of my Python newsletter.

So without further ado, here is the code snippet. Take a moment to reflect on the following dictionary expression and what it will evaluate to:

```
>>> {True: 'yes', 1: 'no', 1.0: 'maybe'}
```

I'll wait here...

Ok, ready?

This is the result we get when evaluating the above dict expression in a CPython interpreter session:

```
>>> {True: 'yes', 1: 'no', 1.0: 'maybe'}
{True: 'maybe'}
```

I'll admit I was pretty surprised about this result the first time I saw it. But it all makes sense when you investigate what happens, step by step. So, let's think about why we get this—I want to say *slightly unintuitive*—result.

When Python processes our dictionary expression, it first constructs a new empty dictionary object; and then it assigns the keys and values to it in the order given in the dict expression.

Therefore, when we break it down, our dict expression is equivalent to this sequence of statements that are executed in order:

```
>>> xs = dict()
>>> xs[True] = 'yes'
>>> xs[1] = 'no'
>>> xs[1.0] = 'maybe'
```

Oddly enough, Python considers all dictionary keys used in this example to be *equal*:

```
>>> True == 1 == 1.0
True
```

Okay, but wait a minute here. I'm sure you can intuitively accept that `1.0 == 1`, but why would True be considered equal to 1 as well? The first time I saw this dictionary expression it really stumped me.

After doing some digging in the Python documentation, I learned that Python treats `bool` as a subclass of `int`. This is the case in Python 2 and Python 3:

> "The Boolean type is a subtype of the integer type, and Boolean values behave like the values 0 and 1, respectively, in almost all contexts, the exception being that when converted to a string, the strings 'False' or 'True' are returned, respectively."[3]

---

[3]cf. Python Docs: "The Standard Type Hierarchy"

And yes, this means you can *technically* use bools as indexes into a list or tuple in Python:

```
>>> ['no', 'yes'][True]
'yes'
```

But you probably should *not* use boolean variables like that for the sake of clarity (and the sanity of your colleagues.)

Anyway, let's come back to our dictionary expression.

As far as Python is concerned, True, 1, and 1.0 all represent *the same dictionary key*. As the interpreter evaluates the dictionary expression, it repeatedly overwrites the value for the key True. This explains why, in the end, the resulting dictionary only contains a single key.

Before we move on, let's have another look at the original dictionary expression:

```
>>> {True: 'yes', 1: 'no', 1.0: 'maybe'}
{True: 'maybe'}
```

Why do we still get True as the key here? Shouldn't the key also change to 1.0 at the end, due to the repeated assignments?

After some mode research in the CPython interpreter source code, I learned that Python's dictionaries don't update the key object itself when a new value is associated with it:

```
>>> ys = {1.0: 'no'}
>>> ys[True] = 'yes'
>>> ys
{1.0: 'yes'}
```

Of course this makes sense as a performance optimization—if the keys are considered identical, then why spend time updating the original?

In the last example you saw that the initial True object is never re-placed as the key. Therefore, the dictionary's string representation still prints the key as True (instead of 1 or 1.0.)

With what we know now, it looks like the values in the resulting dict are getting overwritten only because they compare as equal. However, it turns out that this effect isn't caused by the __eq__ equality check alone, either.

Python dictionaries are backed by a hash table data structure. When I first saw this surprising dictionary expression, my hunch was that this behavior had something to do with hash collisions.

You see, a hash table internally stores the keys it contains in different "buckets" according to each key's hash value. The hash value is de-rived from the key as a numeric value of a fixed length that uniquely identifies the key.

This allows for fast lookups. It's much quicker to search for a key's numeric hash value in a lookup table instead of comparing the full key object against all other keys and checking for equality.

However, the way hash values are typically calculated isn't perfect. And eventually, two or more keys that are actually different will have the same derived hash value, and they will end up in the same lookup table bucket.

If two keys have the same hash value, that's called a *hash collision*, and it's a special case that the hash table's algorithms for inserting and finding elements need to handle.

Based on that assessment, it's fairly likely that hashing has something to do with the surprising result we got from our dictionary expression. So let's find out if the keys' hash values also play a role here.

I'm defining the following class as our little detective tool:

```python
class AlwaysEquals:
    def __eq__(self, other):
        return True

    def __hash__(self):
        return id(self)
```

This class is special in two ways.

First, because its __eq__ dunder method always returns True, all instances of this class will pretend they're equal to *any* other object:

```python
>>> AlwaysEquals() == AlwaysEquals()
True
>>> AlwaysEquals() == 42
True
>>> AlwaysEquals() == 'waaat?'
True
```

And second, each AlwaysEquals instance will also return a unique hash value generated by the built-in id() function:

```python
>>> objects = [AlwaysEquals(),
               AlwaysEquals(),
               AlwaysEquals()]
>>> [hash(obj) for obj in objects]
[4574298968, 4574287912, 4574287072]
```

In CPython, id() returns the address of the object in memory, which is guaranteed to be unique.

With this class we can now create objects that pretend to be equal to any other object but have a unique hash value associated with them. That'll allow us to test if dictionary keys are overwritten based on their equality comparison result alone.

And, as you can see, the keys in the next example are *not* getting over-written, even though they always compare as equal:

```
>>> {AlwaysEquals(): 'yes', AlwaysEquals(): 'no'}
{ <AlwaysEquals object at 0x110a3c588>: 'yes',
  <AlwaysEquals object at 0x110a3cf98>: 'no' }
```

We can also flip this idea around and check to see if returning the same hash value is enough to cause keys to get overwritten:

```
class SameHash:
    def __hash__(self):
        return 1
```

Instances of this SameHash class will compare as non-equal with each other but they will all share the same hash value of 1:

```
>>> a = SameHash()
>>> b = SameHash()
>>> a == b
False
>>> hash(a), hash(b)
(1, 1)
```

Let's look at how Python's dictionaries react when we attempt to use instances of the SameHash class as dictionary keys:

```
>>> {a: 'a', b: 'b'}
{ <SameHash instance at 0x7f7159020cb0>: 'a',
  <SameHash instance at 0x7f7159020cf8>: 'b' }
```

As this example shows, the "keys get overwritten" effect isn't caused by hash value collisions alone either.

Dictionaries check for equality and compare the hash value to determine if two keys are the same. Let's try and summarize the findings of our investigation:

The {True: 'yes', 1: 'no', 1.0: 'maybe'} dictionary expression evaluates to {True: 'maybe'} because the keys True, 1, and 1.0 all compare as equal, *and* they all have the same hash value:

```
>>> True == 1 == 1.0
True
>>> (hash(True), hash(1), hash(1.0))
(1, 1, 1)
```

Perhaps not-so-surprising anymore, that's how we ended up with this result as the dictionary's final state:

```
>>> {True: 'yes', 1: 'no', 1.0: 'maybe'}
{True: 'maybe'}
```

We touched on a lot of subjects here, and this particular Python Trick can be be a bit mind-boggling at first—that's why I compared it to a Zen kōan in the beginning.

If it's difficult to understand what's going on in this chapter, try playing through the code examples one by one in a Python interpreter session. You'll be rewarded with an expanded knowledge of Python's internals.

Key Takeaways

- Dictionaries treat keys as identical if their __eq__ comparison result says they're equal and their hash values are the same.
- Unexpected dictionary key collisions can and will lead to surprising results.

7.5 So Many Ways to Merge Dictionaries

Have you ever built a configuration system for one of your Python programs? A common use case for such systems is to take a data structure with default configuration options, and then to allow the defaults to be overridden selectively from user input or some other config source.

I often found myself using dictionaries as the underlying data structure for representing configuration keys and values. And so I frequently needed a way to combine or to *merge* the config defaults and the user overrides into a single dictionary with the final configuration values.

Or, to generalize: sometimes you need a way to merge two or more dictionaries into one, so that the resulting dictionary contains a combination of the keys and values of the source dicts.

In this chapter I'll show you a couple of ways to achieve that. Let's look at a simple example first so we have something to discuss. Imagine you had these two source dictionaries:

```
>>> xs = {'a': 1, 'b': 2}
>>> ys = {'b': 3, 'c': 4}
```

Now, you want to create a new dict zs that contains all of the keys and values of xs and all of the keys and values of ys. Also, if you read the example closely, you saw that the string 'b' appears as a key in both dicts—we'll need to think about a conflict resolution strategy for duplicate keys as well.

The classical solution for the "merging multiple dictionaries" problem in Python is to use the built-in dictionary update() method:

```
>>> zs = {}
>>> zs.update(xs)
>>> zs.update(ys)
```

If you're curious, a naive implementation of update() might look something like this. We simply iterate over all of the items of the right-hand side dictionary and add each key/value pair to the left-hand side dictionary, overwriting existing keys as we go along:

```python
def update(dict1, dict2):
    for key, value in dict2.items():
        dict1[key] = value
```

This results in a new dictionary zs which now contains the keys defined in xs and ys:

```python
>>> zs
>>> {'c': 4, 'a': 1, 'b': 3}
```

You'll also see that the order in which we call update() determines how conflicts are resolved. The last update wins and the duplicate key 'b' is associated with the value 3 that came from ys, the second source dictionary.

Of course you could expand this chain of update() calls for as long as you like in order to merge any number of dictionaries into one. It's a practical and well-readable solution that works in Python 2 and Python 3.

Another technique that works in Python 2 and Python 3 uses the dict() built-in combined with the **-operator for "unpacking" objects:

```python
>>> zs = dict(xs, **ys)
>>> zs
{'a': 1, 'c': 4, 'b': 3}
```

However, just like making repeated update() calls, this approach only works for merging *two* dictionaries and cannot be generalized to combine an arbitrary number of dictionaries in one step.

Starting with Python 3.5, the **-operator became more flexible.[4] So in Python 3.5+ there's another—and arguably prettier—way to merge an arbitrary number of dictionaries:

```
>>> zs = {**xs, **ys}
```

This expression has the exact same result as a chain of update() calls. Keys and values are set in a left-to-right order, so we get the same conflict resolution strategy: the right-hand side takes priority, and a value in ys overrides any existing value under the same key in xs. This becomes clear when we look at the dictionary that results from the merge operation:

```
>>> zs
>>> {'c': 4, 'a': 1, 'b': 3}
```

Personally, I like the terseness of this new syntax and how it still remains sufficiently readable. There's always a fine balance between verbosity and terseness to keep the code as readable and maintainable as possible.

In this case, I'm leaning towards using the new syntax if I'm working with Python 3. Using the **-operator is also faster than using chained update() calls, which is yet another benefit.

Key Takeaways

- In Python 3.5 and above you can use the **-operator to merge multiple dictionary objects into one with a single expression, overwriting existing keys left-to-right.
- To stay compatible with older versions of Python, you might want to use the built-in dictionary update() method instead.

---

[4]cf. PEP 448: "Additional Unpacking Generalizations"

7.6 Dictionary Pretty-Printing

Have you ever tried hunting down a bug in one of your programs by sprinkling a bunch of debug "print" statements to trace the execution flow? Or maybe you needed to generate a log message to print some configuration settings...

I have—and I've often been frustrated with how difficult some data structures are to read in Python when they're printed as text strings. For example, here's a simple dictionary. Printed in an interpreter session, the key order is arbitrary, and there's no indentation to the resulting string:

```
>>> mapping = {'a': 23, 'b': 42, 'c': 0xc0ffee}
>>> str(mapping)
{'b': 42, 'c': 12648430, 'a': 23}
```

Luckily there are some easy-to-use alternatives to a straight up *to-str* conversion that give a more readable result. One option is using Python's built-in json module. You can use json.dumps() to pretty-print Python dicts with nicer formatting:

```
>>> import json
>>> json.dumps(mapping, indent=4, sort_keys=True)
```

```
{
    "a": 23,
    "b": 42,
    "c": 12648430
}
```

These settings result in a nicely indented string representation that also normalizes the order of the dictionary keys for better legibility.

While this looks nice and readable, it isn't a perfect solution. Printing dictionaries with the json module only works with dicts that contain primitive types—you'll run into trouble trying to print a dictionary that contains a non-primitive data type, like a function:

```
>>> json.dumps({all: 'yup'})
TypeError: "keys must be a string"
```

Another downside of using json.dumps() is that it can't stringify complex data types, like sets:

```
>>> mapping['d'] = {1, 2, 3}
>>> json.dumps(mapping)
TypeError: "set([1, 2, 3]) is not JSON serializable"
```

Also, you might run into trouble with how Unicode text is represented—in some cases you won't be able to take the output from json.dumps and copy and paste it into a Python interpreter session to reconstruct the original dictionary object.

The classical solution to pretty-printing objects in Python is the built-in pprint module. Here's an example:

```
>>> import pprint
>>> pprint.pprint(mapping)
{'a': 23, 'b': 42, 'c': 12648430, 'd': set([1, 2, 3])}
```

You can see that pprint is able to print data types like sets, and it also prints the dictionary keys in a reproducible order. Compared to the standard string representation for dictionaries, what we get here is much easier on the eyes.

However, compared to json.dumps(), it doesn't represent nested structures as well visually. Depending on the circumstances, this can be an advantage or a disadvantage. I occasionally use json.dumps() to print dictionaries because of the improved readability and formatting, but only if I'm sure they're free of non-primitive data types.

Key Takeaways

- The default to-string conversion for dictionary objects in Python can be difficult to read.
- The `pprint` and `json` module are "higher-fidelity" options built into the Python standard library.
- Be careful with using `json.dumps()` and non-primitive keys and values as this will trigger a `TypeError`.

Chapter 8

Pythonic Productivity Techniques

8.1 Exploring Python Modules and Objects

You can interactively explore modules and objects directly from the Python interpreter. This is an underrated feature that's easy to overlook, especially if you're switching to Python from another language.

Many programming languages make it difficult to inspect a package or class without consulting online documentation or learning interface definitions by heart.

Python is different—an effective developer will spend quite a bit of time in REPL sessions working interactively with the Python interpreter. For example, I often do this to work out little snippets of code and logic that I then copy and paste into a Python file I'm working on in my editor.

In this chapter you'll learn two simple techniques you can use to explore Python classes and methods interactively from the interpreter.

These techniques will work on any Python install—just start up the Python interpreter with the python command from the command-line and fire away. This is great for debugging sessions on systems where you don't have access to a fancy editor or IDE, for example, because you're working over the network in a terminal session.

Ready? Here we go! Imagine you're writing a program that uses Python's datetime module from the standard library. How can you find out what functions or classes this module exports, and which methods and attributes can you find on its classes?

Consulting a search engine or looking up the official Python documentation on the web would be one way to do it. But Python's built-in dir() function lets you access this information directly from the Python REPL:

```
>>> import datetime
>>> dir(datetime)
['MAXYEAR', 'MINYEAR', '__builtins__', '__cached__',
'__doc__', '__file__', '__loader__', '__name__',
'__package__', '__spec__', '_divide_and_round',
'date', 'datetime', 'datetime_CAPI', 'time',
'timedelta', 'timezone', 'tzinfo']
```

In the example above, I first imported the datetime module from the standard library and then inspected it with the dir() function. Calling dir() on a module gives you an alphabetized list of the names and attributes the module provides.

Because "everything" is an object in Python, the same technique works not only on the module itself, but also on the classes and data structures exported by the module.

In fact, you can keep drilling down into the module by calling dir() again on individual objects that look interesting. For example, here's how you'd inspect the datetime.date class:

```
>>> dir(datetime.date)
['__add__', '__class__', ..., 'day', 'fromordinal',
'isocalendar', 'isoformat', 'isoweekday', 'max',
'min', 'month', 'replace', 'resolution', 'strftime',
'timetuple', 'today', 'toordinal', 'weekday', 'year']
```

As you can see, dir() gives you a quick overview of what's available on a module or class. If you don't remember the exact spelling for a particular class or function, then maybe that's all you need to keep going without interrupting your coding flow.

Sometimes calling dir() on an object will result in too much information—on a complex module or class you'll get a long printout that's difficult to read quickly. Here's a little trick you can use to filter down the list of attributes to just the ones you're interested in:

```
>>> [_ for _ in dir(datetime) if 'date' in _.lower()]
['date', 'datetime', 'datetime_CAPI']
```

Here, I used a list comprehension to filter down the results of the
`dir(datetime)` call to only contain names that include the word
"date." Notice how I called the `lower()` method on each name to
make sure the filtering is case-insensitive.

Getting a raw listing of the attributes on an object won't always be
enough information to solve the problem at hand. So, how can you get
more info and further details on the functions and classes exported by
the `datetime` module?

Python's built-in `help()` function will come to your rescue. With it,
you can invoke Python's interactive help system to browse the auto-
generated documentation for any Python object:

```
>>> help(datetime)
```

If you run the above example in a Python interpreter session, your terminal will display a text-based help screen for the `datetime` module,
looking somewhat like this:

```
Help on module datetime:

NAME
    datetime - Fast implementation of the datetime type.

CLASSES
    builtins.object
        date
            datetime
        time
```

You can use the cursor up and down keys to scroll through the documentation. Alternatively you can also hit the space bar to scroll down

a few lines at once. To leave this interactive help mode you'll need to press the q key. This will take you back to the interpreter prompt. Nice feature, right?

By the way, you can call `help()` on arbitrary Python objects, including other built-in functions and your own Python classes. The Python interpreter automatically generates this documentation from the attributes on an object and its docstring (if available.) The examples below are all valid uses of the help function:

```
>>> help(datetime.date)
>>> help(datetime.date.fromtimestamp)
>>> help(dir)
```

Of course, `dir()` and `help()` won't replace nicely formatted HTML documentation, the powers of a search engine, or a Stack Overflow search. But they're great tools for quickly looking things up without having to switch away from the Python interpreter. They're also available offline and work without an internet connection—which can be very useful in a pinch.

Key Takeaways

- Use the built-in `dir()` function to interactively explore Python modules and classes from an interpreter session.
- The `help()` built-in lets you browse through the documentation right from your interpreter (hit q to exit.)

8.2 Isolating Project Dependencies With Virtualenv

Python includes a powerful packaging system to manage the module dependencies of your programs. You've probably used it to install third-party packages with the `pip` package manager command.

One confusing aspect of installing packages with pip is that it tries to install them into your *global* Python environment by default.

Sure, this makes any new packages you install available globally on your system, which is great for convenience. But it also quickly turns into a nightmare if you're working with multiple projects that require different versions of the *same* package.

For example, what if one of your projects needs version 1.3 of a library while another project needs version 1.4 of the same library?

When you install packages globally *there can be only one* version of a Python library across all of your programs. This means you'll quickly run into version conflicts—just like the Highlander did.

And it gets worse. You might also have different programs that need different versions of Python itself. For example, some programs might still run on Python 2 while most of your new development happens in Python 3. Or, what if one of your projects needs Python 3.3, while everything else runs on Python 3.6?

Besides that, installing Python packages globally can also incur a security risk. Modifying the global environment often requires you to run the `pip install` command with superuser (root/admin) credentials. Because pip downloads and executes code from the internet when you install a new package, this is generally not recommended. Hopefully the code is trustworthy, but who knows what it will really do?

Virtual Environments to the Rescue

The solution to these problems is to separate your Python environments with so-called *virtual environments*. They allow you to separate Python dependencies by project and give you the ability to select between different versions of the Python interpreter.

A *virtual environment* is an isolated Python environment. Physically, it lives inside a folder containing all the packages and other dependencies, like native-code libraries and the interpreter runtime, that a Python project needs. (Behind the scenes, those files might not be real copies but symbolic links to save memory.)

To demonstrate how virtual environments work, I'll give you a quick walkthrough where we'll set up a new environment (or *virtualenv*, as they're called for short) and then install a third-party package into it.

Let's first check where the global Python environment currently resides. On Linux or macOS, we can use the `which` command-line tool to look up the path to the pip package manager:

```
$ which pip3
/usr/local/bin/pip3
```

I usually put my virtual environments right into my project folders to keep them nice and separate. But you could also have a dedicated "python-environments" directory somewhere to hold all of your environments across projects. The choice is yours.

Let's create a new Python virtual environment:

```
$ python3 -m venv ./venv
```

This will take a moment and will create a new venv folder in the current directory and seed it with a baseline Python 3 environment:

```
$ ls venv/
bin         include    lib         pyvenv.cfg
```

If you check the active version of pip (with the which command), you'll see it's still pointing to the global environment, /usr/local/bin/pip3 in my case:

```
(venv) $ which pip3
/usr/local/bin/pip3
```

This means if you install packages now, they'd still end up in the global Python environment. Creating a virtual environment folder isn't enough—you'll need to explicitly *activate* the new virtual environment so that future runs of the pip command reference it:

```
$ source ./venv/bin/activate
(venv) $
```

Running the activate command configures your current shell session to use the Python and pip commands from the virtual environment instead.[1]

Notice how this changed your shell prompt to include the name of the active virtual environment inside parentheses: (venv). Let's check which pip executable is active now:

```
(venv) $ which pip3
/Users/dan/my-project/venv/bin/pip3
```

As you can see, running the pip3 command would now run the version from the virtual environment and not the global one. The same

---

[1]On Windows there's an activate command you need to run directly instead of loading it with source.

288

is true for the Python interpreter executable. Running `python` from the command-line would now also load the interpreter from the venv folder:

```
(venv) $ which python
/Users/dan/my-project/venv/bin/python
```

Note that this is still a blank slate, a completely clean Python environment. Running `pip list` will show an almost empty list of installed packages that only includes the baseline modules necessary to support pip itself:

```
(venv) $ pip list
pip (9.0.1)
setuptools (28.8.0)
```

Let's go ahead and install a Python package into the virtual environment now. You'll want to use the familiar `pip install` command for that:

```
(venv) $ pip install schedule
Collecting schedule
  Downloading schedule-0.4.2-py2.py3-none-any.whl
Installing collected packages: schedule
Successfully installed schedule-0.4.2
```

You'll notice two important changes here. First, you won't need admin permissions to run this command any longer. And second, installing or updating a package with an active virtual environment means that all files will end up in a subfolder in the virtual environment's directory.

Therefore, your project dependencies will be physically separated from all other Python environments on your system, including the global one. In effect, you get a clone of the Python runtime that's dedicated to one project only.

By running pip list again, you can see that the schedule library was installed successfully into the new environment:

```
(venv) $ pip list
pip (9.0.1)
schedule (0.4.2)
setuptools (28.8.0)
```

If we spin up a Python interpreter session with the python command, or run a standalone .py file with it, it will use the Python interpreter and the dependencies installed into the virtual environment—as long as the environment is still active in the current shell session.

But how do you deactivate or "leave" a virtual environment again? Similar to the activate command, there's a deactivate command that takes you back to the global environment:

```
(venv) $ deactivate
$ which pip3
/usr/local/bin
```

Using virtual environments will help keep your system uncluttered and your Python dependencies neatly organized. As a best practice, all of your Python projects should use virtual environments to keep their dependencies separate and to avoid version conflicts.

Understanding and using virtual environments also puts you on the right track to use more advanced dependency management methods like specifying project dependencies with requirements.txt files.

If you're looking for a deep dive on this subject with additional productivity tips, be sure to check out my Managing Python Dependencies course available on dbader.org.

Key Takeaways

- Virtual environments keep your project dependencies separated. They help you avoid version conflicts between packages and different versions of the Python runtime.
- As a best practice, all of your Python projects should use virtual environments to store their dependencies. This will help avoid headaches.

8.3 Peeking Behind the Bytecode Curtain

When the CPython interpreter executes your program, it first translates it into a sequence of bytecode instructions. Bytecode is an intermediate language for the Python virtual machine that's used as a performance optimization.

Instead of directly executing the human-readable source code, compact numeric codes, constants, and references are used that represent the result of compiler parsing and semantic analysis.

This saves time and memory for repeated executions of programs or parts of programs. For example, the bytecode resulting from this compilation step is cached on disk in .pyc and .pyo files so that executing the same Python file is faster the second time around.

All of this is completely transparent to the programmer. You don't have to be aware that this intermediate translation step happens, or how the Python virtual machine deals with the bytecode. In fact, the bytecode format is deemed an implementation detail and not guaranteed to remain stable or compatible between Python versions.

And yet, I find it very enlightening to see *how the sausage is made* and to peek behind the abstractions provided by the CPython interpreter. Understanding at least some of the inner workings can help you write more performant code (when that's important). And it's also a lot of fun.

Let's take this simple greet() function as a lab sample we can play with and use to understand Python's bytecode:

```python
def greet(name):
    return 'Hello, ' + name + '!'

>>> greet('Guido')
'Hello, Guido!'
```

Remember how I said that CPython first translates our source code into an intermediate language before it "runs" it? Well, if that's true, we should be able to see the results of this compilation step. And we can.

Each function has a __code__ attribute (in Python 3) that we can use to get at the virtual machine instructions, constants, and variables used by our greet function:

```
>>> greet.__code__.co_code
b'd\x01|\x00\x17\x00d\x02\x17\x00S\x00'
>>> greet.__code__.co_consts
(None, 'Hello, ', '!')
>>> greet.__code__.co_varnames
('name',)
```

You can see co_consts contains parts of the greeting string our function assembles. Constants and code are kept separate to save memory space. Constants are, well, constant—meaning they can never be modified and are used interchangeably in multiple places.

So instead of repeating the actual constant values in the co_code instruction stream, Python stores constants separately in a lookup table. The instruction stream can then refer to a constant with an index into the lookup table. The same is true for variables stored in the co_varnames field.

I hope this general concept is starting to become more clear. But looking at the co_code instruction stream still makes me feel a little queasy. This intermediate language is clearly meant to be easy to work with for the Python virtual machine, not humans. After all, that's what the text-based source code is for.

The developers working on CPython realized that too. So they gave us another tool called a *disassembler* to make inspecting the bytecode easier.

Python's bytecode disassembler lives in the dis module that's part of the standard library. So we can just import it and call dis.dis() on our greet function to get a slightly easier-to-read representation of its bytecode:

```
>>> import dis
>>> dis.dis(greet)
  2           0 LOAD_CONST               1 ('Hello, ')
              2 LOAD_FAST                0 (name)
              4 BINARY_ADD
              6 LOAD_CONST               2 ('!')
              8 BINARY_ADD
             10 RETURN_VALUE
```

The main thing disassembling did was split up the instruction stream and give each *opcode* in it a human-readable name like LOAD_CONST.

You can also see how constant and variable references are now interleaved with the bytecode and printed in full to spare us the mental gymnastics of a co_const or co_varnames table lookup. Neat!

Looking at the human-readable opcodes, we can begin to understand how CPython represents and executes the 'Hello, ' + name + '!' expression in the original greet() function.

It first retrieves the constant at index 1 ('Hello, ') and puts it on the *stack*. It then loads the contents of the name variable and also puts them on the *stack*.

The *stack* is the data structure used as internal working storage for the virtual machine. There are different classes of virtual machines and one of them is called a *stack machine*. CPython's virtual machine is an implementation of such a stack machine. If the whole thing is named after the stack, you can imagine what a central role this data structure plays.

By the way—I'm only touching the surface here. If you're interested in this topic you'll find a book recommendation at the end of this chapter. Reading up on virtual machine theory is enlightening (and a ton of fun).

What's interesting about a *stack* as an abstract data structure is that, at the bare minimum, it only supports two operations: *push* and *pop*. *Push* adds a value to the top of the stack and *pop* removes and returns the topmost value. Unlike an array, there's no way to access elements "below" the top level.

I find it fascinating that such a simple data structure has so many uses. But I'm getting carried away again...

Let's assume the stack starts out empty. After the first two opcodes have been executed, this is what the contents of the VM stack look like (0 is the topmost element):

```
0: 'Guido' (contents of "name")
1: 'Hello, '
```

The BINARY_ADD instruction pops the two string values off the stack, concatenates them, and then pushes the result on the stack again:

```
0: 'Hello, Guido'
```

Then there's another LOAD_CONST to get the exclamation mark string on the stack:

```
0: '!'
1: 'Hello, Guido'
```

The next BINARY_ADD opcode again combines the two to generate the final greeting string:

```
0: 'Hello, Guido!'
```

The last bytecode instruction is RETURN_VALUE which tells the virtual machine that what's currently on top of the stack is the return value for this function so it can be passed on to the caller.

And voila, we just traced back how our greet() function gets executed internally by the CPython virtual machine. Isn't that cool?

There's much more to say about virtual machines, and this isn't the book for it. But if this got you interested, I highly recommend that you do some more reading on this fascinating subject.

It can be a lot of fun to define your own bytecode languages and to build little virtual machine experiments for them. A book on this topic that I'd recommend is *Compiler Design: Virtual Machines* by Wilhelm and Seidl.

Key Takeaways

- CPython executes programs by first translating them into an intermediate bytecode and then running the bytecode on a stack-based virtual machine.
- You can use the built-in dis module to peek behind the scenes and inspect the bytecode.
- Study up on virtual machines—it's worth it.

Chapter 9

Closing Thoughts

Congratulations—you made it all the way to the end! Time to give yourself a pat on the back, since most people buy a book and never even crack it open or make it past the first chapter.

But now that you've read the book, this is where the real work starts—there's a big difference between *reading* and *doing*. Take the new skills and tricks you learned in this book, and go out there and use them. Don't let this be just another programming book you read.

What if you started sprinkling some of Python's advanced features in your code from now on? A nice and clean generator expression here, an elegant use of the `with`-statement there...

You'll catch the attention of your peers in no time—and in a good way too, if you do it right. With some practice you'll have no trouble applying these advanced Python features tastefully, and to only use them where they make sense and help make your code more expressive.

And trust me, your colleagues will pick up on this after a while. If they ask you questions, be generous and helpful. Pull everyone around you *up* and help them learn what you know. Maybe you can even give a little presentation on "writing clean Python" for your coworkers a few weeks down the road. Feel free to use my examples from the book.

There's a difference between *doing* a great job as a Python developer, and *to be seen doing* a great job. Don't be afraid to stick your head out. If you share your skills and newfound knowledge with the people around you, your career will benefit greatly.

I follow the same mindset in my own career and projects. And so, I'm always looking for ways to improve this book and my other Python training materials. If you'd like to let me know about an error, or if you just have a question or want to offer some constructive feedback, then please email me at mail@dbader.org.

Happy Pythoning!

— Dan Bader

P.S. Come visit me on the web and continue your Python journey at dbader.org and on my YouTube channel. Also, be sure to get your free copy of the Python Tricks Digital Toolkit available at dbader.org/python-tricks-toolkit.

9.1 Free Weekly Tips for Python Developers

Are you looking for a weekly dose of Python development tips to improve your productivity and streamline your workflows? Good news—I'm running a free email newsletter for Python developers just like you.

The newsletter emails I send out are not your typical "here's a list of popular articles" flavor. Instead I aim for sharing at least one original thought per week in a (short) essay-style format.

If you'd like to see what all the fuss is about, then head on over to dbader.org/newsletter and enter your email address in the signup form. I'm looking forward to meeting you!

9.2 PythonistaCafe: A Community for Python Developers

Mastering Python is *not* just about getting the books and courses to study. To be successful you also need a way to stay motivated and to grow your abilities in the long run.

Many Pythonistas I know are struggling with this. It's simply a lot less fun to build your Python skills completely alone.

If you're a self-taught developer with a non-technical day job, it's hard to grow your skills all by yourself. And with no coders in your personal peer group, there's nobody to encourage or support you in your endeavor of becoming a better developer.

Maybe you're already working as a developer, but no one else at your company shares your love for Python. It's frustrating when you can't share your learning progress with anyone or ask for advice when you feel stuck.

From personal experience, I know that existing online communities and social media don't do a great job at providing that support network either. Here are a few of the best, but they still leave a lot to be desired:

- *Stack Overflow* is for asking focused, one-off questions. It's hard to make a human connection with fellow commenters on the platform. Everything is about the facts, not the people. For example, moderators will freely edit other people's questions, answers, and comments. It feels more like a wiki than a forum.

- *Twitter* is like a virtual water cooler and great for "hanging out" but it's limited to 140 characters at a time—not great for discussing anything substantial. Also, if you're not constantly online, you'll miss out on most of the conversations. And if you *are* constantly online, your productivity takes a hit from the never-ending stream of interruptions and notifications. Slack chat groups suffer from the same flaws.

- *Hacker News* is for discussing and commenting on tech news. It doesn't foster long-term relationships between commenters. It's also one of the most aggressive communities in tech right now with little moderation and a borderline toxic culture.

- *Reddit* takes a broader stance and encourages more "human" discussions than Stack Overflow's one-off Q&A format. But it's a huge public forum with millions of users and has all of the associated problems: toxic behavior, overbearing negativity, people lashing out at each other, jealousy, ... In short, all the "best" parts of the human behavior spectrum.

Eventually I realized that what holds so many developers back is their limited access to the global Python coding community. That's why I founded PythonistaCafe, a peer-to-peer learning community for Python developers.

A good way to think of PythonistaCafe is to see it as a club of mutual improvement for Python enthusiasts:

Inside PythonistaCafe you'll interact with professional developers and hobbyists from all over the world who will share their experiences in a safe setting—so you can learn from them and avoid the same mistakes they've made.

Ask anything you want and it will remain private. You must have an active membership to read and write comments and as a paid community, trolling and offensive behavior are virtually nonexistent.

The people you meet on the inside are actively committed to improving their Python skills because membership in PythonistaCafe is invite-only. All prospective members are required to submit an application to make sure they're a good fit for the community.

You'll be involved in a community that understands you, and the skills and career you're building, and what you're trying to achieve. If you're trying to grow your Python skills but haven't found the support system you need, we're right there for you.

PythonistaCafe is built on a private forum platform where you can ask questions, get answers, and share your progress. We have members located all over the world and with a wide range of proficiency levels.

You can learn more about PythonistaCafe, our community values, and what we're all about at **www.pythonistacafe.com**.

83451763R00167

Made in the USA
Lexington, KY
12 March 2018